Ruthie's Trails
A Lifetime of Adventure

by Ruth Oltmann

Scrambling at Bow Summit above Peyto Lake, Banff National Park, c 1971.

Ruthie's Trails: A Lifetime of Adventure
by Ruth Oltmann

Other books by the author:
The Kananaskis Valley Hikers' & X-C Skiers' Guide
The Valley of Rumours...the Kananaskis
Lizzie Rummel: Baroness of the Canadian Rockies (Rocky Mountain Books)
My Valley ◆ the Kananaskis (Rocky Mountain Books)

Copyright © 2011 Ruth Oltmann

ISBN 978-0-9691716-1-4

Mount Fable Press

Box 32,
Exshaw, Alberta,
T0L 2C0

403-673-3832
ruthieo@telusplanet.net

Pirnted in Canada.

Book layout by Suzan Chamney, Glacier Lily Productions.

Front cover photo: Ruthie on Ruthie's Trail, 1982. Photo: Barbara Snyder.
Unless otherwise noted all photos are by the author or from the Oltmann collection.

To Mark and Julie Kent

who unwittingly were the catalysts for this book.

Angela —
Have fun too

Rudie Oehman?

Acknowledgements

J am especially grateful to Mark and Julie Kent for the gift that started all this, to Peggy Magee for the story of the ducklings, to Janice (Boschman) Kirkman for her relief houseparent report, to Lynda Beyer for her Mount Allan remembrances, and especially to Vi Sandford for scanning my paper copy stories. My sincere gratitude goes to Suzan Chamney for her very able designing of this book and many wonderful ideas, and to Ron Chamney for tweaking and cleaning the cover photo. My thanks also to all the people who have entered my life and enhanced it beyond my wildest dreams.

Contents

Introduction

My life really has been an adventure. When I was a teenager all kinds of crazy things would happen to me, not bad, just different from the norm. I would come home after being out somewhere and my mother would ask me what I did. I would tell her and she would accuse me of lying and give me a really hard time. There was no way I could convince her otherwise, so after a few of those occasions I would just say something innocent like I was at Mary's house. She never questioned that kind of answer. I didn't like to lie to her, but my adventures were beyond her comprehension. That made her happy. Me? I just went on having adventures.

Today if my very conservative mother read this book (she is no longer living) she would be horrified at some of the things I've done. Like rafting the Nahanni River at the age of seventy-two a year after back surgery, or dressing up like I was about to do a winter climb only to be pushing my walker in Bow Valley Provincial Park in -15 C temperatures while I waited for a surgeon to decide what to do with another back problem.

Oh well, what do you do with a girl like.......

Over the years I've written stories and articles from my life. Hiking and skiing stories and lots of other adventures were found in my old Mac computer and my filing cabinet. Once I found them I felt committed to do one more book. Some of these stories have a historical bent because so much has changed in our world and it is good to remember and learn about the past. Some stories are in miles, with elevations in feet, and some are in metric as Canada changed its system during my lifetime. I did all my climbing in feet—the pun is unintentional—and my memory bank has many elevations in it, all in feet. I hope you enjoy my stories as much as I've enjoyed reliving these parts of my life. Even I am amazed at what I did in the mountains.

Chapter 1

In the Beginning

Brian, Ruthie, Kitty, Joanne and Neil Oltmann, c 1941.

Ancestors

Nicolai and Kjersti Johnsrud, my father's parents, emigrated from Norway to Cook, Minnesota, U.S.A., then moved to North Dakota and finally to Castor, Alberta, Canada, arriving about 1909. My father, George Hjalmar Johnsrud, was born in 1910 and was the first of their children born in Canada. Six were born in either Norway or the U.S.A. I don't know what my grandfather did when he first arrived in the United States and Canada, but eventually he became a welder and there is a story he worked on the High Level Bridge in Lethbridge, Alberta.

Tragedy struck the family in 1916 when my grandmother died one week after the birth of her ninth child. Something like toxic poisoning which penicillin, discovered years later, would have prevented. A man with eight children—one had died previously—and one a week-old baby, on the frontier of Alberta, could not work and look after his children. There were no social services in those days, so the children were farmed out to various people. My father was one of the lucky ones as William and Mary Oltmann, who farmed in the Castor area after emigrating from the U.S.A., legally adopted him. My father called his foster parents Uncle Billy and Auntie Mum.

My mother, Beulah Winifred MacKenzie, was born in 1909. Her ancestors originate from Scotland, probably coming to Canada in the 1700s. One of them fought with General Wolfe on the Plains of Abraham (now part of Quebec City). My mother was born in Saint Sixte, Quebec, which is southeast of Ottawa. At that time Quebec was very backward, so the family, who were farmers, moved to the Ottawa Valley and farmed near the Town of Chesterville. The road their farm is on is now called MacKenzie Road as MacKenzie family members have lived there ever since. My mother was still in elementary school at the time of the move and she never did go beyond Grade 8. The family was poor, so she got a job as a housekeeper in Ottawa until she married.

My father moved from Alberta to Ottawa to work for the federal government. My parents were married on December 1st, 1933.

When I was Just a Little Girl

My parents spent the first six years of their married life living in Westboro, which was a village on the west side of Ottawa, but is now part of the city. It was here their first three children were born: Joanne Beth (1934), Kjersti (Kitty) (1936), and me, Charlotte Ruth, on February 27, 1937. There are pictures of us, three little girls and my mother. I am the one with the blond ringlets.

After a few years my parents moved to the *Little House* that my father had purchased. It was on the other side of the railway tracks in Westboro where there were three other houses and an old Indian living in the forest. The area was composed of forest and Tunney's pasture where my father grazed our goats. This area is now a big subdivision, the forest is gone, and there is a huge government complex in the pasture, although it is still called Tunney's Pasture.

My parents George and Beulah Oltmann in Ottawa, Ontario, 1969.

While living in the *Little House* two more children were born—Neil (1938) and Brian (1939). During WWII my father was a pilot, but was home on leave long enough for David (1943) to show up. During the war Daddy was training in New Brunswick and my mother went there to visit him. She had to take Neil, as he wouldn't be parted from her. I was very jealous as I had an itchy foot even at that tender age.

The *Little House* had four rooms—a kitchen, living room and two bedrooms. Four children slept in two double beds in one room and my parents and Brian, the baby, in the other bedroom. It had a pump for water, an outhouse, and wood stove cooking and heating. Daddy built a rock deck on the front of the house. There was also a small barn for the goats.

The old Indian in the forest would come around and scare us children. One of our neighbours, an older girl, would go into the forest and tell him to leave us alone. We thought she was very brave.

School Years

When I was six years old my parents moved from Westboro and bought a house in Ottawa South. This was the year I started Grade One at Hopewell Avenue Public School. It was three blocks away. There was no such thing as kindergarten when I was five. We must have moved in early September because I was a few days late starting school. I remember going to school that first day wearing a little plaid coat and the teacher never told me to take it off.

A few years later my two older sisters and I were standing outside the school talking with a friend who thought we were the only children in our family. There were probably seven of us at the time and I found the idea of only three kids in the family beyond my ability to comprehend. Later when I left home I found I couldn't live in a house without children for several years.

While we lived in Ottawa South two more children arrived. Nancy Ingrid (1946) and Nora Lea (1948). I was nine and eleven years old at the time, so can remember these baby girls very well and helped to look after them; changing diapers, feeding and generally helping Mother. Ingrid couldn't say her name when she was little, so she dubbed herself Ning or Ningy. For years we called her that, but the nickname fell into disuse by me as she got older. Ingrid was a beautiful baby with a thick head of brownish, auburn hair and Nora Lea was a tiny baby (she's still under five feet) with very unruly, curly hair, much curlier than mine.

Eight children are a lot of work and there is no way you can do it all yourself, you have to get the kids to help. Fortunately my mother had three girls first. She taught us how to cook and clean and make beds and look after younger siblings. Saturday mornings had a ritual to them. We were not allowed to go out of the house until two girls made beds, dusted furniture, floors, and baseboards (no vacuums in those days), and the other one washed the breakfast dishes and cleaned up the kitchen. We never argued about doing the work—that was non-negotiable. What we argued about was who was going to wash the dishes as we didn't like that job. Later when we were all grown up my mother said we were better housekeepers before we were teenagers than we were as teenagers.

When I was seven years old I started piano lessons. The lessons cost 25 cents each and were in a class with several other children. I took lessons like this for three years. Afterwards I continued my interest in the piano by playing it at every opportunity. At one time my sister Joanne had a boyfriend who had Grade Ten in music, so I asked him to show me how to do chording. After he showed me a basic chord I developed others on my own. For many years music played a big part in my life—piano and singing.

Grandpa and Uncle Allan

He was our favourite uncle. Not that we didn't like the others, but being the youngest of my mother's siblings Uncle Allan was in our lives longer, and he stayed on the MacKenzie farm in the Ottawa Valley so we saw more of him. He and Grandpa loved to tease us.

When I was a little girl Grandpa used to tell me that if I ducked my head in the barrel of whey that was in the farm yard by the pump it would get rid of my freckles. I would hover over that barrel trying to get up the nerve to duck my head in it, but the thought of those long ringlets full of whey just put me off. Today I can imagine Grandpa hiding behind the barn door chuckling while watching me. It's a good thing I didn't put my head in the barrel as not only would I have been disappointed to still retain my freckles, but I'd have lost faith in a Grandpa I loved.

The barn was a never-ending source of enjoyment to the Oltmann and MacKenzie cousins. We would climb up the ladder to the high beams and jump into the hay below. No one ever got injured as the hay was soft and fluffy. We could spend hours there while the adults visited in the house.

Many years later Uncle Allan, his wife Jean, and my Aunt Evelyn came to Alberta and visited me in Exshaw. I took them up the Icefields Parkway for a tour in the mountains. En route we stopped at Saskatchewan River Crossing and had a picnic lunch overlooking the North Saskatchewan River. We also had a picnic supper at my home overlooking Mount McGillivray and Heart Mountain. Sometime after Uncle Allan passed away Aunt Jean told me how much he loved picnics. Guess whom I take after?

The House that Daddy Built

My father built a cement block house on Highway 31, now Bank Street, when it was just outside the city limits. He had received a Department of Veterans Affairs loan with which he bought two and a half acres of farmland. He did most of the work himself with the help of his two oldest sons, Neil and Brian. He hauled cement blocks in his old Ford car a few at a time; he worked on the house for about a year.

In 1950, when I was 13 years old, we moved into the new, unfinished house. The move was hard on Mother. She had eight children with another on the way—Phillip (1951)—and she didn't want to move. She had a nice circle of friends in Ottawa South and was happy there. However, when she sold the house—long after Daddy died—she realized a sizable amount of money, which set her up financially for the rest of her life.

When we moved into the house it only had the sub floor and the kitchen was unfinished. Mother had a few orange crates that served as a kitchen cupboard set up in a corner of the dining room. We were still in the icebox stage of life, so things were pretty primitive. We had a well in the basement and the septic field out back, on top of which my father eventually planted a huge garden.

The Highway 31 house was one mile from the recently extended city limits of Ottawa. That was as far as the city bus went, so we had to walk that mile if we were going anywhere on our own, but a school bus did stop by the house. As I got older and branched out with my social life, I saw a lot of that one-mile stretch of highway. I often walked it in high-heeled shoes and if my feet were getting sore I took them off and walked in my nylon stockings. In those days there wasn't glass and gravel on the paved roads, so it was easy walking and the smooth pavement felt good on the feet.

We had to walk by the Jewish Cemetery, which was always spooky, and past the small pond with croaking frogs, but the only time I was unhappy about that walk was when I had to walk with Brian. He would torment me mercilessly. Brothers!

The Highway 31 house was a big house for a big family. Six bedrooms, two of which were converted to a den and a spare room as the children grew up and left home. My father once again bought a few goats and erected a single wire electric fence around the grazing area. He built two little barns, one for the goats and one for the hay. The goats' milk and the big garden lessened the financial load of the large family.

The rule was that when I was going steady with a fellow I had to be home by midnight. When I was seventeen I went steady with Ronnie. One night he got me home at midnight, drove off and I went to the front door and rang the bell to get in, as my mother never gave us a key. I rang the bell several times with no result, so I went to the back door and banged on it. No result, in spite of the fact there were ten people in the house! After an hour of ringing and banging front and back doors I gave up and went to the barn where there was a little hay. The goats had long since departed. I took off my light blue spring coat and lay down on the hay and put the coat over me and went to sleep. At six o'clock in the morning Neil shook my shoulder and demanded to know where I'd been. I had a lot of difficulty in convincing my mother of the true story. I'm not sure she was ever really convinced, but I think I got a house key after that. When you grow up in a big family you learn to sleep through anything. I still sleep through anything, including the big snorers in alpine huts.

The Froom Family

When we lived in Ottawa South there was a family living two doors away who had four children, one of whom was a blind and mentally challenged boy. I was often used as a baby sitter and helper for Arnold and Pauline Froom's family and I became like an older child to them. I called Mr. Froom "Froomie" and later I would call Mrs. Froom, Mom.

Pauline Froom had a serious thyroid problem and didn't always have the energy to look after her house and children, so I did a lot of cooking and cleaning and minding the children for her. When I was 12 years old she slipped a disk in her back and was in bed for a week. It must have been summer holidays because I went to the house every day and cooked, cleaned, did the laundry, ironed clothes and looked after three children. The youngest, Robert, came along later. One day I was ironing Froomie's white shirt; when I gave it to him he had a good look at it and said he'd keep his suit jacket on. I've never been able to iron clothes adequately.

Froomie could talk a bird out of a tree. He had a wonderful manner, was a born salesman, and very diplomatic. He had his own insurance business and was very successful. Pauline had a sister living in Cobalt, Ontario, who had gone out with the same fellow for a long time. She was in love with him, but he wasn't proposing, so Froomie suggested she tell the fellow that she thought they should break up; not because she didn't love him—she did, but she felt he should be free to see other women. That did the trick, he didn't want to lose her, so he proposed and they lived happily ever after—really.

When I slept at the Froom house I always had to sleep with Carol, the only daughter. Carol was a restless sleeper and she would snuggle up to me and eventually I would be pushed right over to the side of the bed. When that happened I learned to get out of the bed, go around the other side and snuggle up to her opposite side. She would eventually work me back to the vacant side of the bed and I would have to repeat the manoeuvre. I guess it's called adapting. When Carol was a baby I taught her to take her first steps. Today she is married with several grandchildren. She and her husband own the famous Patterson Berry Farm south of Ottawa.

David, the blind child, was a genius in music. He could play anything he heard on the piano perfectly. He would sit on the couch for hours, rocking back and forth, with music going on in his head. Then he would get up, go over to the piano, sit down and play the pieces. The first time he heard Chopin's Chopsticks he didn't play the piano for a week. Just sat on the couch and rocked back and forth. Then he got up, went to the piano, and played it note perfect. By the time he was twelve years old a man had written down fifty pieces David had composed.

For five years David went to the School for the Blind in Brantford, Ontario. One time I took him on the train back to the school. Five years later David could remember the exact day of the week and date that I had taken him. He was a genius in remembering dates. He only got to Grade Five, but David was a very special child and I thought he was wonderful.

After Brantford school David was put in a section of the mental hospital in Brockville, Ontario. His parents wanted him to adjust to institutionalization in preparation for the day they would no longer be able to look after him. They knew it would be easier for him to adapt when he was young and straight from the Brantford school. My brother Davy was training as a psychiatric nurse in that hospital and he said that David thought he was still in school. One of the patients in the mental section had been a teacher and he took it on himself to teach David. Also, *Sing Along with Mitch* (Miller) was popular at the time and David would play the piano and the patients would sing along. They called it *Sing Along with David*. If David leaned back and clapped his hands and laughed in his joyful, childish laugh, no one thought he was strange. He did more good for the patients in that institution than many people on the outside did.

An Accident

When I was seventeen, I borrowed a bicycle and took Carol Froom and a friend of hers to the beach for the day. As I was turning into the beach area I made a wide turn to accommodate Carol coming up behind me. I missed the drive over the culvert and went into the ditch, flew over the top of the bicycle, plowed the earth with my face getting a mouthful of dirt, breaking my hand and receiving a concussion. I ended up with amnesia and didn't know where I was and why I was there. The young girls had to dig in my pocket to get the dime to call Carol's parents. Froomie came and got us and took me to the hospital where I had my hand x-rayed and put in a cast. He took me back to their house and I stayed with them a whole month—until my talking straightened out.

School Stuff

Mathematics was a difficult subject for me. I never did very well, except once. In Grade Eight I received 100 per cent on a math problems test. I was the only one in the two Grade Eight classes who received 100 per cent. The teacher made a big deal out of it. I was as surprised as she was.

There was no junior high in those days. Elementary school went to Grade Eight and then you were in high school. I went to the High School of Commerce because my parents said I wasn't smart enough to go to the collegiate where Joanne and Kitty went. Grade eleven was boring me and some of the other students were telling me how hard it was, so I asked my parents if I could get a job. They were not that strong on the value of education, so I left school at the age of seventeen and got a job as a stenographer in downtown Ottawa.

More Education

I had been working for about a year and a half at the stenographer job and, while I didn't have much money, I gathered what I did have and enrolled at Central Baptist Seminary in Toronto in a non-degree two-year English Bible course. I was eighteen years old and had never been away from home. I knew I had to get a part time job to support myself, as my parents clearly couldn't do that. At first I tried a couple of housekeeping jobs, but that didn't work out, so I got a job as a typist five afternoons a week since I only had morning classes. I rented a housekeeping room and did all my own cooking on a two-burner grill with two orange crates as my kitchen cupboard. Having a room all to myself after sharing with sisters all my life was wonderful.

A social butterfly existence and student life were difficult to mix together, subsequently I failed my first year in seminary. I got an office job for the summer and started back the following September. By this time I'd gained a bit of maturity and was doing okay. Disaster struck when I became very sick and ended up in hospital for two weeks and had to convalesce for a month. This meant I had to go back home, as I had no money. When I got better I got a job in the Ottawa Civic Hospital where I had been born and where the Dutch princesses had been born during World War II.

I went back to seminary in 1957 for my third try at year one in the same course. Over the next two years I managed to complete the course and graduation day on May 4, 1959, was the happiest moment of my life. My father was proud of me and came to Toronto for my graduation. Mother, of course, was home with the younger children.

Summer Camp

The summer I finished seminary I went to work at Round Lake Bible Camp, 55 miles (88 km) from Fort William and Port Arthur (now Thunder Bay). It was a small camp with only two female counsellors for the girls' camp. There was a very straight-laced couple managing the camp. One day I was having a nice chat with the fellow doing the laundry and they thought we were up to something naughty—I think we were complaining about them. June, the other counsellor, was engaged to Carl who worked with a Christian organization in the area. Carl came to visit June and brought along his buddy Mike. They knew about a waterfall across the lake and the two guys convinced us to get up in the night and row across the lake to see it. We had to be very careful that no one heard us, especially the straight-laced couple. It was a hazy moon so we could see where we were going, but not so bright that we'd be noticed. The waterfall was lovely. We rowed back and went to bed and no one was ever the wiser. At the end of the summer I was June's Maid of Honour when she married Carl.

After the summer at the children's camp, I worked as a stenographer and legal secretary in Toronto until the end of 1963.

My graduation from Central Baptist Seminary, Toronto, Ontario, 1959.

15

Go West Young Lady, Go West

A new beginning dawned in 1964 when I made plans to work my way west across the country. I didn't want to spend the rest of my life in Toronto and it was time to follow my star. In January I went to Lively, Ontario, where my sister Joanne was living with her family, and spent a month with her and her husband Earl and two children. In my travels I always chose the cheapest mode of transportation—bus or train. From Lively I went to Winnipeg. I rented a room and got a job for a month.

While on the train I had fallen and injured my back so that I limped as if I had one leg shorter than the other. One of the Office Overload jobs I had was with a Jewish company. When the boss discovered that my limping was from an injury he sent me to a relative who was the best orthopedic surgeon in Winnipeg. He did a lot to help me and never charged me a cent—long before Medicare.

The room I rented had a view of the Golden Boy on top of the legislative building. One of the roomers was a French girl with whom I became friends. She matched me up with a French fellow and we did some double dating. One time we went to a restaurant that served alcohol. When we walked in the door the waitress wanted to see my I.D. (I was twenty-seven years old). When I showed it to her she nearly fell over and didn't ask my nineteen-year-old friend for hers (the drinking age was twenty-one years at the time). That, of course, was the story of my life; looking ten years younger than I was. Although I didn't drink I wanted to be with my friends and was always asked for my I.D., up to and including age thirty-one. After that I wasn't asked anymore, after all, by then I looked twenty-one!

My French friends took me to their hometown, La Broquerie, south of Winnipeg, for a weekend. It was a totally French town. I remember attending a Catholic church that was all in French and Latin.

While my new friends wanted me to stay in Winnipeg and date this fellow, I still had to follow my star west, so I moved on to Regina where I spent another month. I lived in the YWCA and got another Office Overload job, but I didn't like Regina as I didn't find the people as friendly as Winnipeg.

Calgary was next and I got a two-month job with a couple of lawyers. While on a city bus I bumped into an old friend from Ottawa who was a legal secretary. Through Joan's encouragement I applied and got a job in the law office where she worked. However, before I started I took a month and went to Wrangell, Alaska to visit a friend. Unfortunately, the job was short-lived as my boss was difficult, so I quit and got an executive secretarial job with two men who had numerous businesses, including four nursing homes. I worked and lived in Calgary for six years.

At this time my Oltmann grandparents were still living in Castor, Alberta, so I often visited them and my pseudo aunt, Colleen Coleman, and her family. My Oltmann grandparents had unofficially adopted Colleen thirteen years after my father had left home. Her mother had also died and left several children. Colleen was six months old when they took her in.

Colleen was a go-getter. She had about three jobs at once. One of them was grading eggs. We did a lot of visiting in the egg-grading shack. One day I mentioned I wanted to buy a car, so we went to the only car dealer in town and before I knew it I had purchased a 1952 Dodge with low mileage for $150. Its previous owner was a farmer who only drove it on Sundays. I didn't have a driver's license, so when I got back to Calgary I got a learner's permit and the next weekend I got a ride to Castor with a couple of Colleen's friends, who were drinking and driving all the way to Castor, while I hung on in fear. I drove my car around and, with one of the fellows accompanying me, drove it all the way back to Calgary myself. The next week I got my driver's license. The following month I drove to Prince Rupert, B.C. and took a ferry to Wrangell, Alaska. At the time I was living with an elderly lady, Annie Colley, who was an old friend of my father's. Her son told me I had more guts than brains to do that drive. He was probably right.

The Yellowhead Highway was pretty wild in those days. There was no connection between Jasper, Alberta, and Prince George, B.C. You had to drive to Cache Creek, B.C. and north to Prince George. The latter town had a bar on every corner and I was in a cheap hotel feeling very insecure the night I stayed there. There was nothing from Terrace to Prince Rupert—some natives who lived in the forest, but no towns and no habitations along the road. There was one picnic site and I was planning on stopping there for lunch when I realized I was being followed by a couple of fellows in a car. My old Dodge wouldn't go faster than fifty miles an hour (80 km/h) and it was a winding road, so I did a lot of praying and just kept driving. Finally the guys got tired of the game and drove past me and I never saw them again.

In Prince Rupert I left my car in storage and took the ferry to Wrangell. During my visit my friends took me in a small motorboat up the Stikine River to a venison roast. The deer was roasted on a spit over an open fire. The meat was delicious.

After this month long trip I returned to work in Calgary.

Chapter 2

The Canadian Youth Hostel Association

On the trail to Rockbound Lake, Banff National Park, 1967.

Introduction to Hostelling

*I*n early 1967 I was still working in Calgary. For two years the owners of the compan-
ies I worked for operated their office out of the Mayfair Nursing Home. I came
to know the nursing home staff and patients well and thought they were delightful.
Sing-Along with Miss Ruth became a monthly occurrence.

Mrs. Freeman, who was recreation director for the nursing home, kept insisting
that I join the youth hostel association. All she knew about it was that the members
had work parties fixing up hostels. To satisfy her I went to the hostel office one evening
in February and paid my ten dollars and became a member. After that I attended the
Thursday night social evenings and, when hiking started in the spring, I went along
with the outdoor group.

When I started with the hostel association I was a real neophyte in the mountains.
The following story is taken from my book *My Valley ♦ the Kananaskis.*

The car bumped and rattled over the dirt road at a speed far too fast for
the potholes. I barely had time to look at the scenery while I held onto my
seat. I wasn't sure I wanted to be here with this mad driver, and anyway what
was a hostel work party?

The crazy driver and I were going to Ribbon Creek Hostel in the
Kananaskis Valley for a hostel work party, and would be meeting up with a
group of seasoned Calgary hostellers. The hostel was the old A-frame building at the time and it was my first hostel experience. As it turned out, it was
fortunate I was a heavy sleeper and never noticed the infamous pack rats
(a.k.a. wood rats).

We arrived on a Friday night in May 1967. The next day everyone got
involved in various projects. There were still some bits and pieces of the old
coal-mining village around and I remember going with one of the fellows to
salvage some of the lumber to add to the hostel. While we were wandering
through the site I stepped on a nail that went right into my foot. While I
managed to extricate my foot, it eventually became infected, so I spent the
weekend nursing it, and the next week soaking it in the kitchen sink. Since
I wasn't much help after that, Geoff Spedding amused me by taking me out
in his four-wheel drive Land Rover. We bumped and lunged over the rocks
of Evan-Thomas Creek, but all I remember are the big boulders and a hazy
glimpse of Mount Kidd while I hung on with yet another crazy driver.

No one told me what kind of food hostellers took to eat when at a hostel,
and my boyfriend didn't tell me either, so on Saturday night when we brought
out the strawberries, shortcake and whipped cream everyone made fun of
us, but I was too inexperienced to get the drift. I expect there is a lot more
strawberry shortcake eaten today than in those days. People were pretty basic
with the food they brought.

For the July long weekend I was invited to go with a party of eight on an overnight backcountry trip. I didn't know much—if anything—about it. I knew enough to invest in a good down sleeping bag and a foamie to sleep on. I still had my two dollar and thirty-nine cent pack that my roommate Ursula Lehmann (now Hutchinson) and I had each bought so I used that. It was a sack. No frame, no padded straps and no hip band.

What I didn't know then, but found out later is that it was really a climbing trip to the Royal Group of mountains in British Columbia. We drove endless kilometres on B.C.'s logging roads, then left the cars and started hiking. This was B.C. bush—big trees and steep slopes. I struggled to keep up. The first day consisted of traversing steep snow slopes and climbing up onto huge fallen trees and down the other side and don't lose sight of the group. After several hours we arrived at Queen Mary Creek where we were able to hop across. Then a decision was made. Three of us didn't have ice axes (whatever they were) and couldn't go up the intended mountain—Mount King George. So, we three had to stick together and take two days to hike out via a different route from the one we came in on, while the rest went to climb the mountain and were to hike out in one day. I remember Kathy Forest (now Calvert) was along as the only other girl. I was left with Ron somebody and Don Campbell—two guys I'd never laid eyes on before.

We had a memorable hike down Queen Mary Creek to the Palliser River. I had to share a two-man tent with these two tall guys. I didn't understand the ethics of male/female tent sharing at that time, but this is what happens and what happened that first night. I was allowed to get in the tent first and in my sleeping bag which was placed between the two guys' bags. Not having slept in a down sleeping bag before I thought I would be cold, so I left all my clothes on, including my wool sweater. Then the guys got in after they had hung our food bag in a tree a long way from the tent.

In the morning Ron, who was a very quiet, tall seventeen year old, got up and sat on a big rock in the sun looking at the scenery. Don kept saying he was going to get up every time I said I was going to get up, but he kept rolling over. Finally, I just got up, as I was hot in that down bag with all those clothes on and with the sun on the tent. Later I came to understand that the guys would always let the girls get in the tent first and in the morning get up before the girls in order to give them privacy.

Fifteen times in three days we had to cross Queen Mary Creek. This was the July first long weekend and it was spring runoff. At first we could jump across the creek, but we were going downstream, so it became deeper, wider and faster. There were also several avalanche slopes to cross with snow on them from old avalanches. I was always bringing up the rear and at one crossing one foot broke through the snow and my leg went down a hole. After a quick scramble up I looked back and saw the packed snow was only about one or two inches thick and the hole looked down to the creek about fifteen feet below. I didn't have time to be scared as I had to catch up to the guys.

We had several fords of Queen Mary Creek and then ran into a rock wall and deep water at a major ford. Don didn't think we'd make it across, so he and Ron spent two hours felling two trees with a small hatchet. When that was done they roped me up with Ron on one end of the rope and Don at the other and me in the middle. Ron walked across in the water hanging onto tree branches. He was well over six feet tall.

When it was my turn I had to do the same while the guys kept the rope taunt. Halfway across I was in water up to my waist and my feet were swept from under me. I heard Don yell "Pull the rope, pull the rope." I had to pull myself up onto the tree trunk and crawl through the branches. When I got across Don followed.

By the time we got to the other side it was dark so Don said we had to camp. The guys got a fire going and I hid behind a tree and put dry clothes on. At 103 pounds and five feet six inches tall it was easy to hide behind a tree! Once the guys got changed they cooked up a big pot of rice over the fire and we ate. The next problem was where to sleep. There was no place to put a tent, so we just put our sleeping bags among the rocks in the only place available and crawled inside.

As I lay in my sleeping bag and looked up past those huge trees to the stars above my only thought was: "This is what I've always wanted."

The next day was a continuation of the epic. From there on I was always roped up for creek crossings as the water got deeper and faster. I had no experience fording fast water, so didn't know how to brace myself against the current, plus I was totally unfit and the pack and I didn't weigh very much.

The last creek crossing was very wide and very fast. Ron took one end of the rope, and Don put the other end around a tree and gave it to Ron who then walked through the stream to the other side with the two rope ends. Then Don tied the two of us together, put us between the two sections of the rope and then hooked us onto the rope with carabiners. He put a pole in my hand and one in his and we started across using the poles for balance. When I started to lose my footing he put his hand on my shoulder and pressed down with all his strength to give me traction. We did make it, but it was a tight go.

At one point during these creek crossings I started feeling bad that Don was lumbered with this neophyte and that I was a drag on the two of them. Gradually I

Randy, Dennis, Ruthie and John atop Castle Mountain (previously called Mt. Eisenhower), 1967.

came to realize that he was enjoying figuring out how to get this lightweight across the creek. Later I discovered he was a physics teacher!

By the time I got home I was a physical basket case, but the very next weekend I was out backpacking with the hostel group again and never stopped. Interestingly, that next weekend I met Mary Hawkins who married Don Campbell a year later. We've been friends ever since.

My first rock climbing was with the Calgary hostel group and was a rock school on the cliffs below Mount Yamnuska with Don Vockeroth as guide along with amateur leaders. I remember that Peter Greaves (a.k.a. Pete the Beard) started climbing beside me when I first went up the cliff. Right away he saw I knew where to put my hands and feet, so he went back down and said, "Oh, a natural." After that I did several big—but not difficult—climbs with the group.

This was the beginning of my involvement in the hostel association—hiking, climbing, ski touring, and downhill skiing for the next three years.

Three Guys on a Hike

The Plan: hike up Carrot Creek, over the height of land, and down to Lake Minnewanka, hike to the east end of the lake, ford the Ghost River and hike west along the lake trail to the Minnewanka boat launch. All in two days!

The three guys were Mike English, Jim somebody and another guy, whose name I forget, and me. It must have been late June or early July because Carrot Creek was so high we had to link hands for stability as we forded in thigh deep water. This was the late 1960s prior to the age of walking poles. All went well until we were over the height of land. The stream down to the lake was small, so we mostly jumped across it, however, at one point I jumped across onto what I thought was moss on rock, only to discover it was moss on water. Down I went into the stream and bashed my knee on a rock. The fellows very kindly took some of the weight from my backpack and I hobbled down to the lake where we set up camp.

The next morning we hiked east to the outlet of the lake where the Ghost River starts only to discover the water was too high to ford. The fellows asked a boater who was handy to take us across the lake, mentioning my injury. The boat owner was kind enough to also take us a long way up the lake. This turned out to be fortuitous.

As we hiked Mike and the fellow whose name I forget decided to go faster and hike ahead so they could hitchhike back to the car at Carrot Creek and bring it to the boat launch. In the process they discovered the distance was much further than we realized—no Gem Trek maps with mileages on them in those days and no trail guides—so they contacted a warden who was in the area and they came with him in his big boat down the lake to rescue me and Jim. The warden was just about to launch his small boat so he could get into the shore to pick us up when the park superintendent came along in his small boat and offered to get us and take us to the warden's big boat.

The superintendent nosed his boat into the shore and told me to crawl onto the front of the boat. Once there he said, "Put your arms around my neck and I'll swing you over the windshield." As soon as I did this Mike said the warden rubbed his hands in glee and said, "I'm next." I was still a sweet young thing at this time. However, the superintendent didn't do as he said, he just roared back up the lake, with the warden in hot pursuit, to the boat launch and dumped us there and took off around to the park warden's dock.

When the warden arrived at the dock he rushed right by the sweet young thing and went straight for the park superintendent's throat.

Spray River Hostel

In 1970 when I lost my job with a commercial land appraisal company, someone said "Why don't you run a hostel for the summer?" I ended up going to Spray River Hostel, which is four kilometres from Banff up—what is now called—the Spray River Trail. You had to hike or cycle to get to it.

Before moving to the hostel, one bright, sunny Alberta day, Dick St. Hilaire and I hitchhiked to Banff and hiked into the hostel. We found it wasn't in great shape, but a little paint and soap and water would make a definite improvement. We decided to con some friends into making up a work party to clean the place. Neil Worley, an executive member of the Mountain Region section of the hostel association at that time, promised to put in gas lights, a gas burner and a sink—a little civilization!

The hostel consisted of four small cabins: a male dorm, a female dorm, a common room, and a houseparent (manager) cabin. It had wood stove heating and propane cookers in the common room, but not in the houseparent (manager) cabin.

The first week at this hostel my friend Gerry Johnson and his young friend Russ came to see me. At Gerry's suggestion Russ made me a sign in the form of a wooden triangle with a hand tooled maple leaf on it with the words *Ruthie's House*, and in the corners the letters CYH. A triangle with a maple leaf was the hostel emblem at that time. Little did he know that the sign would be prophetic. From then on everyone called me Ruthie, and I ran hostels for the next eight and a half years.

Journal Entries

Thursday, May 14, 1970

Here I am in the hostel, firmly entrenched, and enjoying myself. I arrived this past Sunday, Ursula and Len Hutchinson brought me up as I overslept and missed my ride with Don and Geoff. Dick, Martin, Mark and Diana came as well and helped me settle in, or at least clean up after some clods broke in and left the place a pig sty.

I didn't expect to meet anyone for some time, so on Tuesday I walked into town to shop. After arriving back at the hostel I was just making a late lunch when a young, blonde girl arrived to have a look at the hostel. Marilyn likes to hike and works at a cafe in Banff for the summer. She also came on Wednesday and we went on a hike and met two young fellows. We had a nice chat down at the den, about three miles up the fire road and they came back here for tea. However, the boys missed out on the tea as I had a terrible time getting the fire going and they had to get back to the Banff Springs Hotel where they work. I expect to see them again.

During the early evening I was sitting with the door to my cabin open when a young fellow arrived by bicycle and stated he came to chop some wood for me. Marilyn had sent him – a friend of hers from the Bank of Montreal and university. We didn't get any wood chopped, but Rini Boers and I did have a nice visit and cup of tea.

This morning I decided to hike into Banff and do a bit of shopping and get the axe sharpened before the hippies started coming and possibly causing trouble. I met two girls on the fire road and gave them directions to the trail to the hot springs and invited them to drop in any time.

We had snow on Tuesday morning, about one inch, and everything was just beautiful. All that snow is gone, but there are still some big patches from the winter, however, it gets warmer every day and I get more used to being alone every day. The peace and tranquility is seeping into my being and making me feel good.

I now have my cabin fixed up nicely with red and white checked curtains and oilcloth tablecloth to match as well as oilcloth on the counter and one shelf. It certainly makes the place look cheery and homey, especially with the wood stove burning away and me chopping wood like mad. Of course, the only amenity resembling civilization is running water, only it's running in the river!

I guess all this extra labour keeping a household going really is wearing as I go to bed about 9:30 p.m. and don't get up until 7:30 a.m.

Tuesday, May 19, 1970

Things sure have happened since the last installment. Thursday night Dan and Mayer arrived from Montreal – no gas for the stoves in the common room so I had them cooking in my cabin. Then Friday night Morton, a friend of theirs from Montreal, arrived. Dan and Mayer are quiet, but Morton is rather chatty.

Saturday morning Russ arrived with the sign he made me saying *Ruthie's House*. It is just gorgeous and I now have it hanging on the wall in a prominent place.

Sunday evening people started arriving in great bunches—all fellows, including two from Ottawa. Russ fixed up the Coleman stove to work with the white gas I had so I didn't have the lot cooking in here. However, they all meandered in later in the evening and sat around talking. Sunday morning Rini was to come back to chop wood—he came Saturday morning, but the axe had been lost on Friday night. When Rini arrived Sunday morning he had come to stay overnight, so he, Russ and I bushwhacked to the little trail behind the hostel, followed it to the hot springs and down to the Banff Spring Hotel where we had tea and then took the fire road back to the hostel.

The Case of the Missing Axe

Friday night Mayer and Dan went out to the woodpile to chop wood with the axe I had sharpened the day before. They chopped wood all right, but they left the axe outside while they were in having supper and when I went out later to get the axe, to make some kindling, it was gone. We all looked for it Friday night and then again on Saturday morning but to no avail, so Dan went to Banff to buy a new axe, to which he and Mayer donated two dollars and thirty-nine cents, the rest being paid by me from hostel funds. We used the axe extensively all weekend and on Monday morning we found the old axe partway under the boys' dorm at the back. My suspicion, of course, was that the boys camping down the road had come along and stolen it, returning it when they left on Monday or Sunday night. So, here we are with two axes and the mystery unsolved.

Monday morning Russ, Rini and I decided to go climbing up Sulphur Mountain and before we knew it we had two fellows eager to come with us and two more eager to come up the high trail to the hot springs. We charged up the hill behind the hostel until we came to the trail and the cairn we had marked the day before and then onto an avalanche chute where we left the two fellows who were en route to the hot springs. We climbed up the avalanche chute—scrambling up snow and little cliffs until we hit a really big cliff. I got carried away and started climbing up the rock and pretty soon everyone else was doing the same, including Paul who wasn't quite sure he wanted to continue whenever he got tired. We sat around in wood tick infested ground eating our sparse, shared cheese sandwiches and cookies before scouting around for an easy way down. It was considerably easier than the way up, but it was very steep and we had to be careful of our footing. We all made it without casualty down to the trail. Paul said he was quite interested in going up Mount Rundle sometime this week! That's what a little climb up a mountain does for people – spurs them on to other mountains.

Last night, Monday, before Rini left (Russ, Paul and Brian had left us at the trail after the climb) Mayer and Dan arrived back at the hostel with Dan a little sick. This morning as they were finishing the breakfast dishes a young lady arrived—my first girl hosteller, Linda. She has just gone off to the dam and little lake about three miles down the road and plans on coming back via the hot springs trail and bushwhacking down from the cairn. She arrived back after hiking to the warden's cabin having missed the lake turnoff.

In the interim I finished the laundry I was doing and also washed my hair that hadn't been washed in a week and a half and also made some tea biscuits.

Eisenhower Hostel

During my time at Spray River Hostel I cycled to Eisenhower Hostel (now called Castle Mountain) to see Mrs. Florence Spear who, at that time, had been manager there for nineteen summers. I had often stayed in this hostel in the winter with the Calgary hostel group. However, there was a big difference in the summer. Mrs. Spear had the place spotless.

By the time I got back to Spray River Hostel I was thinking that the hostel should always look that clean and there should be a manager in the winter too. The more I thought about this the more I felt I would like to be that person.

One Sunday with this on my mind I had a strong feeling I should write a letter to the Hostel Association and suggest it. There had never been a winter hostel manager before in any of the mountain hostels. The feeling was so strong that I sat down and typed up a letter, including the fact I would need to be paid. (My summer at Spray River Hostel was as a volunteer.) One hour later Don and Mary Campbell walked into the hostel to see me. Don was president of the Association at the time. I showed him

Eisenhower Hostel, Banff National Park, 1971.

the letter. He read it and said, "Done!" However, it did have to be voted on at an executive meeting, but that was not a problem.

In September I moved to Eisenhower Hostel (a.k.a. Ike Inn) and spent two years there, but not in July and August, as I would not presume to take Mrs. Spear's place. I was paid 75 dollars a month. During the two summers I got a job as cook at Skoki Lodge in the backcountry from Lake Louise.

Only One Year

What is it like to tell of a year?
Of a year that is not quite done,
Of its hectic days and quiet ways,
And the rising and setting sun.
The month of September is travellers and friends,
Friends who are planning great hikes.
The hikes are a flop because of the snow
The old woman of Eisenhower knows.
September rings out and October rings in
To the tune of school children's howls.
The honeymooners try for a night all alone,
But someone comes in in a cowl.
The Boston climber arrives on the scene,
To find himself late for the climb.
The girls' dorm gets a paneling
From two nice ski boys
A Chicagoan, Norwegian work hard.
It's Santa Claus time and they all do arrive,
It's twenty-four people for dinner.
The pudding is done and the wine is set out,
And everyone eats a great winner.
The New Year rings in with a quieter air,
And February is just the same.
The paintbrush goes mad during February month,
And March brings the skiers insane.
The sun shines in April, but rain comes down too,
The skiers continue on through.
Easter is high school and nattering Ruthie,
Clean up you beggars clean up.
University's all over and travelling begins,
Of hippies and hostellers and others.
It's only one year, but it's gone oh so fast,
Its rewards are too numerous to utter.

—Ruthie, 1971/72 Eisenhower Hostel

Assets and Liabilities

There are assets to being a hostel manager, but there are also liabilities. Some of the assets are obvious, such as being in the mountains constantly, which includes a peaceful life (most of the time), clean fresh air, having a crazy cat and your own homemade bread, and company when you want it (and sometimes when you don't), having large Christmas dinners and, not the least of which is having a cup of tea most anytime.

The liabilities are not always as obvious, but they are there nonetheless. Lack of sleep during large group weekends, and Christmas can become a major liability, especially when you try to snooze in the afternoon and get interrupted. Sitting on hoar frost in the biffy is known to all, but rearranging what's down under to make room for more is seldom known. Then, of course, you have the cheapskates who want a free hostel or you have more people than you can even fit on the floor. Getting people to do a hostel duty can also be a bit of a chore, but then so can washing sheets by hand. Lack of funds is an obvious liability, but running out of propane at -20 F isn't always thought of.

On the whole the assets and liabilities balance quite evenly, but something more is needed to make one want to stay in the wilderness. It isn't easy to know what that something is, even if you are the one involved, but maybe it is the ability to wander through the woods in the summer and make your own cross-country ski trails in the winter because, not only do you discover various birds and animals, but unexpected meadows standing regally on their own, become poignant, and 1920 cars that speak of an age long gone appear mysteriously in the woods. By far the greatest attraction to me is the peace derived from the beauty of the land. When I stop for a minute to rest while breaking a new ski trail the tranquility of the scene reaches to the depth of my being and nothing else in the world matters.

It doesn't really matter what makes one flee the city smog for the clear, crisp air of the mountains, what does matter is how you cope when you get there and I hope that I have learned to cope effectively.

If ever I should leave thee, oh mountains, I shall take with me the feeling of

Bernie Summerscales, Ruthie, and Ron Hopf atop Mount Castleguard in the Columbia Icefield, 1969.
In the background are Mount Columbia (left), and The Twins.

assimilation to the good earth which gives me a sense of deep quiet joy that cannot be equalled and the sense of being part of the land day after day does something good to my soul.

Three Guys in a Pool

Three male friends (I'd best omit names) came to the hostel for a weekend, but were not into a big adventure. One of them suggested we drive to Radium Hot Springs and soak in the hot pool. After sitting in the pool for some time one of the guys said, "Let's go into the cold pool." I entered the pool first and promptly swam towards the deep end. Suddenly I realized the guys were not following me, so I turned around and there they were, three big guys standing in the shallow end of the pool with their mouths hanging open. It turned out that only one of them could swim and for some reason they all assumed I couldn't. Why they wanted to go into the cold pool if they couldn't swim is quite beyond me.

After that whenever they would tease me about their climbing exploits I would just say, "But I can swim."

Three Guys in a Pub

Once a week during the fall and spring I would cycle to Banff to buy groceries, get books from the library, and buy any items I required before cycling back to the hostel at Castle Junction. When my supply of flour was running low I would get a ride from hostel friends so I could buy 50 pounds of flour as I made all my own bread and baked goods.

One day another three male friends gave me a lift to Banff and I bought my flour supplies. Afterward they wanted to go to the Cascade pub. Sitting in the pub drinking beer Doug became verbally abusive to me; maybe because I didn't drink and he drank a lot. Eventually I was completely fed up with his abuse, so without saying a word I stood up, picked up my newspapers and small purchases and put them in one arm, then picked up a glass of beer and much to his surprise, poured it over his head. As I walked out of the pub I could hear the people in the pub clapping. I hitchhiked back to the hostel and when the guys returned Doug apologized. He knew he deserved it.

Hippies

In the early 1970s young people called hippies were travelling across Canada on a shoestring. The ones from the west coast were going east and the ones from the east were going west. Drugs and bumming accommodation were prevalent. I was frequently asked for free accommodation, but the hostels I ran were not free. They were the princely sum of one dollar a night and later two dollars a night. Those who were not willing to pay couldn't stay. I didn't give free overnights as I was working for a mere pittance and I'd have been inundated with freeloaders. A lot of interesting travellers did stay and paid for their overnights.

Because I was a woman alone at the hostel sometimes things bordered on getting out of hand. I could tell by the sound in the Common Room when something had to be done to curtail any potential shenanigans. I would then pick up my axe, walk through the Common Room past the hostellers and out the front door to the wood pile that was in full sight through a big window. I always chose logs without knots in them and proceed to whack them into smaller pieces until I had an armful. I was pretty good at swinging that axe and splitting the wood at one go. With my armload of wood, and axe in hand, I would walk back through the Common Room that was now deadly quiet. There were no problems after that. No one was going to meddle with a woman who could swing an axe like that!

Skoki Lodge

As I mentioned, I did not look after Eisenhower Hostel during July and August. In the winter of 1971 I had a weekend off, so Leslie Moynihan and I, and two guys, Geoff and Ivan, skied the eight miles (13 km) into Skoki Lodge with the understanding that one could stay in one of the cabins and do their own cooking for one dollar a night. This was the wrong information, but by the time we got there and found out, it was too late to ski back, so Bert and June Mickle fed us dinner and allowed us to sleep on the lodge couches in our sleeping bags. We emptied our pockets of money, but it wasn't much.

While chatting with Bert and June we discovered they had all their staff for the coming summer except for a cook. Leslie turned to me and said, "You can cook." That's how I came to cook at Skoki Lodge during the summers of 1971 and 1972.

In those days it was cooking on a wood stove with piped water from a spring on Skoki Mountain. That stove was so big I could bake eight loaves of bread at a time. It took one hour to heat up the stove in the morning, so I was up at 6:00 a.m. and to bed at 9:30 p.m. I met many delightful people, including a science fiction writer and her retired United States admiral husband, and a couple of Lizzie Rummel's former guests at Assiniboine who always insisted I do a hike with them. On my days off I hiked all the trails in the area.

While I was at Skoki my youngest brother, Phill, hiked to the lodge to see me via Baker Creek (in two days) and camped nearby. I took him up Skoki Mountain behind the lodge. In his pack he carried a cast iron frying pan with which to cook over a fire. He told me he would always carry a cast iron frying pan. However, many years later when we hiked into Elbow Lake (1.3 km) in Kananaskis Country he said he would do the cooking and produced a light-weight frying pan. First he cooked the main course in the pan, then the soup, and then made the tea, but never washed the pan! I guess he discovered that his pack could get very heavy.

Gray Creek Hostel

S ometime in the 1970s while travelling I stayed in the Gray Creek home hostel on Kootenay Lake in British Columbia. Old Mrs. Lymbery (I use this term as there is a younger Mrs. Lymbery) was still alive, a widow, and a delightful character.

Sitting in her dining room chatting with me she said that she had seen King George VI and Queen Elizabeth in 1939 when they were in Banff. She reached across the table to a pile of photo albums and produced the one of this event. This intrigued me. Had this album been sitting on her table for over thirty years?

That night her cat kept trying to get inside my sleeping bag. Since the cat was obviously pregnant I didn't let her, even though a warm, cuddly cat would have been welcome in other circumstances. The next morning I woke to little squeals and found the cat had had her kittens on the chair at the foot of my bed.

At that time Mrs. Lymbery's son Tom was running the general store, cabin rentals and camping. He was still doing that at age seventy-eight when I drove by and stopped at the store in 2007. I didn't meet him as he was up the hill with a chain saw cutting trees!

The Gray Creek Store is the oldest family run store in British Columbia. Mrs. Lymbery's house is still there, along with the rustic cabins and the store is a major seller of chainsaws and wood stoves.

From: "Tom" Lymbery
Date: May 23, 2007
Subject: Kathleen Lymbery

Thank you for your email and your memories of my mother, Kathleen. You stayed at a Canadian Youth Hostel in Gray Creek in what year? We had joined CYH because of the interesting people it brought to us—one of the first was a couple on a tandem bike, with a two year old in a trailer behind— from England. They had cycled all the way from Halifax, when much of the highway was still gravel.

My father, Arthur Lymbery came to Gray Creek in 1911 to grow fruit, which he did until his death in 1969.

Kathleen came to Canada in 1920 and they met here and were married in 1920. Kathleen had joined the Women's Land Army in the 1914-18 war in England and was persuaded to come to Kootenay Lake by a fellow worker, Mrs. Gooch, who, with her husband, had established a home in this area in 1912.

Ribbon Creek Hostel

A s mentioned previously, being involved in the hostel association means you participate in hostel work parties. That is what brought me to the Kananaskis Valley the second time – to help work on the foundation for the new Ribbon Creek Hostel. It was in the fall of 1969 when I had my arm in a cast after having broken it in the Bugaboos, so I was carrying rocks for the foundation with one hand.

The third time I went to the Kananaskis Valley was for the opening of the new Ribbon Creek Hostel in 1970. I was hostel manager at Spray River Hostel, but I didn't have a car. Rini Boers said he would come with me and we got a ride from one of his friends and were dropped off at Dead Man's Flats, across from the Grizzly Bar. We camped overnight on the trail and started hiking at six in the morning and planned to be at the hostel in time for the opening festivities and free dinner at suppertime. Canmore Mines was still operating and we managed to hitch a ride for a few kilometres on the back of one of their pick-up trucks. It was a wild and hairy ride; sitting on top of and hanging onto oil drums as we careened around sharp, rising corners on a narrow, rough road. We were unceremoniously dumped at the actual trail, not very far from tree line, at which point we were on our own. We didn't know much about the trail even though I had asked a lot of people for information. The most I found out was where to start and that it was 18 miles long. We discovered the actual mileage when we got to the summit of the mountain as there was a big sign stuck in a cairn. Although it was partially eaten by chipmunks, we could still read that it was eight miles to Dead Man's Flats and five miles to Ribbon Creek (12 km, 8 km).

Due to our early start and the shorter mileage, we had plenty of time to lie on the rocks on the summit and enjoy the view, take pictures and eat the last of our food.

The hike down the mountain to the hostel did not take long and we arrived around four in the afternoon. Pip and Alex Buchanan were the hostel managers at the time and were more famous for owning a monkey than Pip's bike ride from Spray River Hostel to the Banff hospital to have a baby. While waiting for the hostel people from Calgary to arrive with the free dinner we had a great visit, unfortunately, the free dinner never did arrive as the official opening had been postponed. Neither the Buchanans nor I had a phone in our respective hostels, so we could not be notified. Pip and Alex fed me and

Ribbon Creek Hostel, Kananaskis Country, 1973.

Rini and after all these years I still owe them a dinner in return! But that may never happen as they went back to Tasmania. I did have a short visit from them at my home in Exshaw many years later, but they couldn't stay for dinner.

At one point in the evening I lay down in the dorm for a few minutes, but when I heard Marion Elliott I got up and walked into the kitchen and promptly passed out! I'd gotten sunstroke—that taught me to wear a hat when I'm hiking.

At the time Rini was a university student working for the summer at the Bank of Montreal in Banff. Rini's banking career eventually took him to Toronto where he became vice-president of human resources for the head office of the Bank of Montreal, and other exploits; while within two years of our hike, I found myself back in the Kananaskis Valley.

It was in the fall of 1972 when Ribbon Creek Hostel, in what later became Kananaskis Country, required a new manager and I asked for a transfer. Its indoor plumbing was very appealing. I came to love Kananaskis and was in this hostel for six and a half years. This was the commencement of a long career of Kananaskis adventures. I didn't plan it that way, but I would not have missed it for the world.

Jan Boschman, whom I met when she stayed in the Ribbon Creek Hostel, became a good friend and since she was only doing substitute teaching she came to the hostel often and we did a lot of hiking and skiing together. Once when I went away for some reason she looked after the hostel for me and gave me this report when I returned.

Relief Houseparent's Report

January 21 - 28, 1978.
Ribbon Creek Hostel or Coping in a Hostel Environment by Jan Boschman

Saturday

Shortly after you left, I opened the door and Creekie rushed in with a chickadee in her mouth. Naturally, I turned directly to the Manual, but could find nothing on "Birds, Dead" or "Wildlife, Consumption of in Houseparent quarters", so I fell back upon my own discretion and put her outside with it. Another area your Manual could deal with is "Smoke Detectors". The 136th Scouts fried hamburgers for supper!

This morning a man came up onto your porch and peered intently at something, then walked away. I had frozen motionless like a curlew to avoid detection, but as soon as he left I had to run out to see what could interest him so much. He was examining the case of beer bottles. There are 43 here tonight.

Sunday

You were prophetic when you said Ribbon {the cat} might cause some trouble. He was annoyed at being kept in here all night, and didn't accept the inevitable quietly. He must have been walking on the floor-sleepers in the Common Room, because not long after I had let him out of your room, Ron brought him back and asked if I would keep him. Then he knocked my alarm clock off the stool, and in the flailing and fumbling the alarm was turned off. I shot out of bed at 7:40 a.m., but fortunately many were already up. They were out by 10:10 a.m.

Last night one little beggar set a pot, half full of peas and carrots in cooking water, down on the pot shelf with another pot on top. He left a ladle sticking out of it, and it was this I noticed on the morning round. I pulled the ladle out to put it away thereby knocking the pile over and spilling the whole mess. After mopping up, I spotted one of the leaders outside and let him know so he could tear into the kids. I didn't do it with your flair, though.

Two boys came in at 9:00 with a broken binding and asked if they could come in for a bit and make coffee while they mended it. I hesitated, but they had hostelled here before, and most of the cooking was done, so I let them in and charged 50 cents each. Not knowing where to record it, I didn't, and you can enter it wherever it goes.

Rick Smith from Crossfield, still on crutches from an August sky jumping accident, came to see you and discuss a school outing.

Tuesday

I decided to come out tonight after school rather than tomorrow morning. It's been snowing steadily for twenty-four hours in Strathmore, and I drove here in record slow time, dreading this Kananaskis road. But you haven't had any snow and the road is as clear and safe as can be. Outside I can hear water dripping from the eaves.

I'm glad I was booked to teach for both Monday and Tuesday, because if I had gone all the way back just to teach Monday it would have been a wasted trip as school was cancelled for a funeral. I would have been furious with no one to be furious at. The only one I could blame would, by then, be safely beyond my reach.

Only Val and Bruce here Sunday and Monday nights, and she took him back to Calgary this morning.

Wednesday

I scrubbed, waxed, and polished the floors this morning, stopping now and then to rush to a window in a vain attempt to photograph a woodpecker that was hammering on the building. Polishing completed, I switched off that machine and stood back to admire my handiwork. I was quite dissatisfied with the results, but had no intention of redoing it. Robert Warren School should effectively camouflage any streaks tomorrow night.

I don't like housecleaning but often find that once I start I just keep on going. That is my only excuse for what I did next. I got carried away and stole what is probably one of your favourite tasks. I vacuumed the mattress boxes in the Girls' Dorm. Out of all that disgusting garbage I salvaged: two pencils, two pens, eleven rubber bands, two buttons, one unopened chocolate bar (which I ate), a folding comb and brush, matches (they were playing with them in there), ruler, 18 cents, an earring, safety pins, thumbtacks, a cheap ring for a little girl, and a bobby pin with a squirrel on it. Perhaps you've guessed that my real reason for taking on the job was that I suspected there might be money in there!

After scrubbing toilets, I settled down with a cup of coffee, a length of wire, and your father's lamp. I succeeded in pushing and drawing the wire through, but then didn't know if the attached cord was the one you wanted in or the one you had removed.

We've three people here tonight. They say it has been snowing in Calgary all day and the highway is not good, but we've had nothing here. The trails could use some help after the heavy use on the weekend.

One of the fellows lit a fire and shortly after that I discovered the lever to open the flue! I was frantic lest that infernal buzzing start up again.

Thursday

Last night I awoke to the sound of pounding on your door and someone calling, your name, and this around midnight. Moving quite briskly although still essentially asleep, I found my robe and a light and opened the door to a couple who looked very surprised and certainly had no need of the informative "I'm not Ruth" I offered them. They were friends of yours from B.C. and really disappointed at missing you. They decided to go see Phill instead, but hadn't his address. Very clever even in my sleep, I found it for them in the registration book and they left. A fleeting thought crossed my mind as I sank back to sleep that this was an odd time of the night to be travelling. Not until this morning did some questions occur to me: One, how long did I actually stand chatting in the doorway before I finally invited them in? Two, did they perchance not know that they could stay here? Three, who were they? I'm sorry I didn't handle things better. {They were Ruthie's brother Brian and his wife.}

The hostel today is permeated with the odour of wet wood. Continued thawing has resulted in large puddles under the McDougall family room window, in the dining room, and at the join between the kitchen and Boys' Dorm. I have dishpan hands from wringing out rags.

The propane man came today while I was somewhere up Ribbon Creek. I'm not sure, but I think it was one of last night's hostellers who initialled the invoice.

We had just a taste of snow this morning around nine, but it didn't last long. The trails are still iced and fast, Ribbon Creek Trail has some rocks showing along the way at some points.

Robert Warren School arrived, thirty kids and four adults, about 5:00 p.m. I took a cheque. One of the leaders has been here before, and he really made a point of stressing rules to the kids. They didn't have cards with them, so I was busy rounding up forms and cards to fill out when someone remarked that the school had been here last week. I assumed, I hope correctly, that the numbers of the cards recorded for that stay could apply. They are well behaved, but towards the end of the evening entertainment one of the taller boys came dancing into the Common Room and he knocked down your mobile. That sobered everybody down instantly. Ken and I did a very temporary patch-up job and re-hung it, but

I want to leave it as is until you can direct a proper repair.

I noticed some wood chips in the snow at the corner on the end of the Girls' Dorm, and closer examination revealed a woodpecker's handiwork. Yesterday I kept hoping he'd come back so I could get a picture, and now I'm wondering how one discourages woodpeckers.

Ribbon has been sort of whiney and keeps sharpening his claws on furniture. I think he's emotionally upset. None of my Psych courses prepared me for feline counselling.

Friday

It has been a quiet day here. Robert Warren School got up at 6:00 a.m. and were cleaned up and gone two hours later. I got up with them, to be on top of things, and it sure makes for a long day.

I was beginning to think I could go to bed at ten, but just at nine a party of three arrived. Two of them were here last weekend (and slept on the floor) and must have enjoyed it because they turned their GP's in for memberships and sold another friend on the idea.

Dave Gill's group of seven has five minutes to arrive before I lock up.

It started to snow early this morning and kept up until the afternoon. Yesterday's wax didn't work... Oh YUCK! A bloody fly just suicided in my tea. How dégoûtant!

The bucket and rags could be put away today, as there was no problem with leaks. I had begun to think yesterday that you might soon be able to relax your vigilance and stop worrying about the floor because the 700 dollars worth of tile would be curled up and peeled off.

I have a question. Looking about I found rakes and nails, shovels and pails, sandpaper, varnish and stain, barbecue, wires and old rusty pliers, but where do you keep your handsaws?

I believe I over watered your Baby Tears today, for I discovered a big puddle on top of the desk. Some of the papers on top got damp. I am so thankful the water didn't run off and onto all those papers you have piled up.

A poem came to mind as I was larking about in the snow. Perhaps you've heard it too.

Two legs to take me where I'd go,
Two eyes to see the sunset's glow,
Two ears to hear what I would know.
Lord forgive me when I whine,
I'm blessed indeed the world is mine!

I sure like the smell of that liquid paper. And by the way, I had nothing to do with the disappearance of your red felt pen. Blame your fellow house-parents for that.

Two Bats Not in the Belfry

It was a quiet night without any hostellers and I was peacefully reading in my room with my two cats, Ribbon and Creek. Suddenly two bats flew down the chimney in the common room and came straight through the hostel into my room. I turned out the light and opened the back door and one flew out. The other bat clung to the wall above the back door and wouldn't budge. I was frantic and didn't know what to do. Just as I was at the desperate stage someone knocked on the front door of the hostel. When I answered it a man in a neat, plaid shirt asked for some simple directions that I gave him. Just before closing the door I asked him if he knew how to get rid of bats. He came into the hostel and asked for a little box and a piece of thin cardboard. He placed the box over the bat and slid the cardboard along the wall under the box. Carefully holding the two items together with the bat inside he went out onto the back deck and let the bat go. Then he went on his way.

There I was in what was at that time an isolated area of Kananaskis, a woman alone, and this man came along at just the right moment and solved my problem. Who was this mysterious man?

Troll Falls

Don Gardner was hired by the hostel association in 1973 to cut a cross-country ski trail. While looking for a possible location he discovered a beautiful waterfall and named it Troll Falls. He cleared a trail from the hostel to the waterfall and it subsequently became very popular. The trail now starts from the Ribbon Creek parking lot via Skogan Pass Trail and Ruthie's Trail (my trail named by Gardner) and it is even more popular.

One evening I hiked to the falls and sat under the overhanging cliff just enjoying being there. As it was starting to get dark I stood up and scrambled down to the bottom of the falls. Just as I reached the bottom a huge piece of the cliff crashed down onto the very spot where I had been sitting. Someone was definitely looking after me!

A Houseparent's Prayer

Adapted from a prayer by Marjorie Holmes.

*Oh, Lord, sometimes I feel it's all too much—my menagerie, the hostellers, my French
lessons, my weaving, my writing, this houseparent job.
The hostel cleaning is always ahead of me.
No matter how hard I work there is always more to do.*

"I need help," I cry, but no help comes, or it is brief.
No, no, it's all up to me, and when I fail I despair of myself.
And the hostellers, Lord.
I am so often cross and unreasonable with them.
But sometimes they drive me to distraction.
Why do they misbehave?
Why do they want to wear their wet and muddy boots inside?
Why don't they try harder?
I try to be a good houseparent, and this is what I get.
And my animals, Lord. Just when I get my hostellers settled down they start fussing.
It's all too much.
Where is the joy?
What happened to those bright and happy days?
Responsibilities must have crowded them out.
They began to slip away so gradually I didn't even miss them.
But I do miss them, acutely at times.
I grieve for happiness and joy with my hostellers.
And perhaps so do they. So do they.... God, thank you for that thought.
Bless my hostellers and let us see the good in each other, for their sake, as well as mine,
let the ties of duty and habit be changed to something, richer.
For their sake, as well as mine, drive out the evils of discontent.
Lord, bless this hostel and let me see its beauty in disorder.

Bless these Hostellers—their healthy bodies, their lively minds, their dearness.
Bless my job. Let me be equal to it and fulfilled in it.
Above all, bless this hostel family that you have put together in these surroundings
for me to love and take care of.

—Ruthie

Today I'm still a life member of the hostel association that now goes by the name Hostelling International, and I still use hostels.

Most of these mountain hostels are now more luxurious than in the 1970s. When I was manager at Spray River (which no longer exists) and Eisenhower (Castle) it was outhouses and water from the creek and wood stove cooking for me, although Eisenhower did have electricity and propane cookers for the hostellers. Ribbon Creek (now called Kananaskis Wilderness Hostel) had indoor plumbing, propane cooking, electricity, and a shower for the manager, but not for the hostellers, although they do now.

It was a different era then and although I sometimes made mistakes, I did do some things right, and was known for running a clean hostel. I wouldn't have missed it for the world.

Chapter 3

The Environmental Sciences Centre

Main building of the Environmental Sciences Centre.

Research Centre

ixteen kilometres north of Ribbon Creek Hostel in the Kananaskis Valley, the University of Calgary had established a research centre in 1966 across from Barrier Lake. It was here that I worked on my first history book of the Kananaskis Valley: *The Valley of Rumours…the Kananaskis*. On January 1, 1979, I left Ribbon Creek Hostel and moved into a small room at the research centre with my German Shepherd, Kelly, and two cats Ribbon and Creek, and my little publishing company (Ribbon Creek Publishing Company) to work as part time and relief cook. My long association with the people at the Centre made for a smooth transition. Living in a community of thirty people after being in a community of one was a little harder.

Of course, I continued to hike and cross-country ski and was involved in my usual mountain activities with several people while there, including Judy Buchanan who met and married Mike Mappin while they were both working there. Judy, Mike and I did some hikes together and once Judy and I slept in my tent on Barrier Lake's beach.

When head cook Pearl Williams retired, I became head cook.

There were a lot of fun activities at the Centre.

Judy Buchanan in Long Canyon, north west fork of Porcupine Creek, 1979.

Journal Entries

Eau Claire Campground

Kananaskis Valley, Monday, June 18, 1979 – sunny and warm – shorts weather
I woke up this morning where I was camped at Kananaskis Lakes to the tune of road building equipment on the other side of Pocaterra Dam – the Smith-Dorrien Creek Road construction. I had a leisurely breakfast consisting of one boiled egg and two cups of tea. Then I drove north to Hood Creek and hiked up the north slope and up Hood Valley with my German Shepherd Kelly. Eventually I got stopped by cliffs that Kelly couldn't negotiate and I probably shouldn't. Kept high on my way back and had lunch really high. Found a nice easy way down. The mountain slope was really steep and going up was hard. I often wondered why I was doing it, however, I was glad to see the end of the valley, which looked very enticing. I was trying to get to the end when I got hung up on the cliffs. Coming down was hard on the legs and feet due to the steepness. Oh for a nice mountain trail. When I got back to the truck Kelly and I put our feet in Hood Creek and I also washed my face. How good that felt. Drove to this campground and before I got a space I saw Becky, the campground girl, so I made tea for us and we had a nice chat. After Becky left I crocheted for a while. Started a fire and when it got going I made dinner. The usual steak, oh yummy, and macaroni, peas and cheese. Kelly ate the end of the latter mixed with the steak juice. While I was making the fire I ripped one of my fingers on the grate rather badly. I cleaned and bandaged it and since it hurt I took a 222.

It is lovely and pleasant here. I feel really leisurely and lazy. Just before 8:00 p.m. I went for a walk, first for water where I came upon a little trail along the Kananaskis River to Rocky Creek; then Kelly and I went upstream and back through the campground. En route we discovered a trail leading to the government camp. The trail surface appeared very old. In some places it was pack trail width, and others quite narrow. This area was burned out in 1936 and it is possible that the trail predates the fire and was used for a while, but before new growth had really got anywhere. Then we found a bit of the 1936-built road and an old picnic table. In our wanderings we discovered that there are only two other occupied campsites. We all must like to be alone because we are all far apart. When we got back from our walk we crawled inside the truck for rest and relaxation.

Kananaskis

Tuesday, June 19, 1979. Sunny and Cloudy
Had a leisurely morning in the campground, cooking my breakfast over an open fire. I left the campground about noon and drove north. Stopped at the old ranger station and visited Reid and Cathy Campbell. Had a long visit

with Cathy, then stopped at the research centre for a few things and drove into Canmore. Did some shopping and then went over to Lizzie's {Rummel} where I got her out of bed—did not mean to. We had a cup of tea, then I took her shopping and we went to Ziggs for supper. We drove around the new subdivision to see it and then I took Lizzie home. I drove home and went to bed by 10:30ish.

Porcupine Creek

Sunday, June 24, 1979. Sunny and warm with white clouds.

Got up at 8:30ish and was in the kitchen by 8:45 a.m. Served up brunch at 10:00 and Cher and Mike expected brunch but had not told me and I didn't have enough for them. Mike got mad and left in a huff. We had a nice brunch and I really did not have enough for them. Worked all day. Made four pans of squares, two different kinds. Also made chocolate éclairs for supper dessert and paprika-dill pork chops. Yummy. Saidah said she liked everything about all the meals. Judy Buchanan and Mike Mappin had gone over Mount Allan with Barb Zailo and Frank Tester, and they sure enjoyed a dinner the moment they got back. Saidah helped me with the cleaning up, then I finished packing my pack and Judy, Kelly and I took off with Mike in my truck for Porcupine Creek and our backpack trip.

Judy Buchanan on the ridge above Porcupine Creek, Kananaskis Country, 1979.

Mike took the truck back to the research centre and Judy and I hiked up the creek about 1.5 hours. We found a small spot, just large enough for the tent in the trees, shortly after the underground creek resurfaced. It is lovely and quiet with only the creek, mosquitoes and birds for sounds. It is now 10:15 p.m., so we will be crawling into the sack in a minute.

Meadows above Old Mill Road

Monday, June 25, 1979. Sunny and warm

We got up just before 9:00 a.m. I made breakfast while Judy took the tent down. We got packed up and were off at 10:50 a.m. I should mention that about 4:00 a.m. during the night Kelly got up and went for a walk. Shortly after getting back in the tent he started woofing and wanted out. He left barking loudly and his barks echoed from the mountainsides. He eventually came back tired and hot and had obviously had a lie in the creek. I made him sleep outside since he was wet.

This morning we got slowly up Long Canyon and then up the treed slope of the ridge to the north. I wrote it up in my hiking book. We hiked to the top of the ridge we were on and then down to the col and down into the valley below to the meadows where we planned to camp.

We found a small stream and made tea and lolled around. I was really tired and Judy was a close second behind me. After a rest and later dinner we pitched the tent and then walked down to look at the cabin we had seen from up on the ridge. It was a Kananaskis forestry cabin in fine shape – clean and neat, with a melon and tomato on the table. We speculated on the latter as they were fresh.

We got back to our camp and made hot chocolate and I wrote up my journal and my hiking book with our route in it. The flies and mosquitoes are really bad. We could hardly eat and write.

Kananaskis Centre

Tuesday, June 26, 1979. Sunny and very Warm

I got up at 7:50 a.m. and washed at the creek before Judy got up. We had our breakfast with only one cup of tea as it was getting hot and there were no good shady areas. Kelly had the only small spot there was. After breakfast we hiked to the top of the meadow and to the top of all the meadow areas, in order to look into the valleys to the north for possible routes down to Lusk Creek.

When we got back to camp we took the orange tent down, which we had left up in order to see our campsite during our descent. We hiked down to the cabin where we made tea, and then back to the research centre—first on the trail from the cabin, then the Old Mill Road. When we reached the old mill site, at the end of the trail, we removed the flagging and post someone had erected as we wanted to keep the cabin a secret and we felt that anyone who went there should not need to make it so easy to find.

We got to the research centre just after 3:00 p.m., and lay on the grass in the shade by the Girls' Dorm, where we took off our boots and socks and rested.

Three Isle Lake

Monday, July 16, 1979. Sunny and warm

From my Upper Kananaskis Lake campsite I got up about 9:00 a.m. and on the trail at 10:55 a.m. Had lunch at the junction of the trails. The new trail sure is nice to hike on. It saves a lot of time. The slog up to the lake from the Forks sure was hard today. 1,300 feet in 3 km! I had to rest a lot. I think the cooking job, being on my feet all day, tires me more than I realize. However, I made it here and found a nice campsite near a little stream, with a view of the mountains, although not much of the lake. I had a nice welcome rest first, then tea. Kelly crashed as well. There is even a real biffy here!

After supper I took a little walk to the other end of the lake. I was tempted to go up to the top of South Kananaskis Pass, but resisted because I knew I'd get tired on those uphills.

Sure is a nice evening—lovely and quiet, no civilization except for an occasional plane. There are two tents further along from my camp. Had a wee rest and a hot chocolate when I got back to my campsite.

Three Isle Lake

Tuesday, July 17, 1979. Sunny and hot

A blue sky no clouds day. I got up at 7:30 a.m. and by 9:45 a.m. I departed camp for a walk around the lake and up the Northover Valley. It only took an hour to get there. I walked between two humps and sat around on the top of one and enjoyed the view. It was lovely. Kelly and I took a leisurely walk back down the valley, walking on some snow occasionally. Then we walked around the other part of the lake and onto the trail back to camp.

After a short rest I had lunch and Kelly had a milk bone. Then, after I had some tea, I read the book *Getting into Print*. Two hikers from Beatty Lake passed by me while I was reading.

After dinner I put my gear in the tent and my food up the tree and hiked to the top of South Kananaskis Pass. I was reluctant to go to Beatty Lake because of the effort to come back up again.

While I was eating dinner two people arrived and camped just across the lake from me. Then a group of kids, plus two leaders, went by and spent several hours near the other campers. I am not sure if I have leprosy or B.O. No one seems to stop here! Oh well, it is nice to have the peace and quiet.

I found a tree by the campsite with a piece of tin nailed to it; scratched on it were the words, *Sinclair Trail 1854 East Kootenay Historical Ass. Bill & Joe M__mack. A.W. Hunter July 28, 1964.*

Kananaskis

Wednesday, July 18, 1979. Sunny and hot

Got up at 7:20 a.m. as I could hear the kids from the group nearby and was afraid they would come over to the biffy and see my pack in it. It was just as well because it meant I was hiking by 9:45 a.m. Got down to the Forks in about an hour. At the Forks I saw several people coming and going to both lakes and out to civilization.

I turned off the new trail onto the old trail and hiked to the Upper Kananaskis River crossing, where I traversed the river using a log jam. Kelly wouldn't swim because it was deep and fast, so I took my pack off (I had carried his over) and went back and led him across the logs. He did really well. We came upon the new trail being built around the Upper Kananaskis Lake and I walked over to the crew's camp to visit Freeman, however, he was not there. I was tired so had my lunch and made tea and rested for two hours. I talked with the cook before she lay down. Freeman never did show up, so at 2:45 p.m. I hiked out to the trailhead. Took Kelly down to the lake for a cool-off swim and then drove straight home to the research centre and made it in time for dinner.

Kananaskis

Saturday, August 11, 1979. Some rain, sunny and warm.

Worked today. Linda Jones and Saidah Din told me that I had to be the person to get Allan Legge, the research assistant, out to the Centre for his birthday party. About 2:30 p.m. I phoned him and told him that the fridge had quit working and no one was around. Marcia and Peter Wallis, Saidah and Linda had gone to Banff and I didn't know when they would be back—probably late.

Allan had me check fuse boxes and told me to put the milk in the cooler. He said he would be out after he mowed his front lawn. In the meantime, I got everyone going and we decorated the lodge and wrapped up crazy presents (including one of Frank Tester's fenders). Allan called me about 4:30 p.m. to say he was going to have a bath and then come out.

We increased our activities and thought up new ideas. Dave Savage said I should get in a wedding dress and into a box. After some deliberation I relented and Marcia brought down her wedding dress and Cindy Savage her veil. Peter Van Eck put on Cindy's black graduation gown and Eric Carlstrom got a shotgun and redneck cap.

Eventually, after a lot of waiting, Allan was spotted driving in the road. Rick's brother John helped me into the big box and they closed it up and put a big bow on top. Allan came in and got a big happy birthday greeting from everyone and Mike Youso dropped a big box of Styrofoam chips on top of him from the loft. Allan immediately hollered "Ruthie!" – I was busy laughing in the box. Someone told him he had to open his presents starting with the big one. He had guessed that I was in the box, but when he opened it and saw me in a wedding dress he nearly fell over. After a minute he hollered, "Where's Ginny?" Ginny and Dennis Jaques had gone to town.

Well, I stood up and Pete started taking pictures and Eric and Peter Van Eck came forward with their shotgun, Bible and robe. I couldn't say a word. I laughed a lot and couldn't get the grin off my face and Allan laughed a lot too.

Someone put Mandy Wallis in my arms and someone put Jeremy Savage in Allan's arms. Everyone laughed a lot while Pete took pictures.

For years after that party we had a running joke wherein Allan called me wifey—until he married Indra Harry, another researcher.

In January 1980 I had a strong feeling I should save my money. I didn't know why I should do that; however, I followed my feeling and saved as much as I could for six months. That wasn't hard to do as my cook's job had my meals and apartment as part of the salary. By June I realized I didn't want to spend the rest of my working life cooking twelve hours a day so I resigned my cook's position and moved into a small three-roomed cabin 10 miles (16 km) south of Sundre, Alberta, and worked on weaving projects, also intending to do some writing.

Chapter 5

The Alpine Club of Canada

Ruthie behind Leslie Jaquette on the summit of Mount Athabasca, Banff National Park, 1998.

Joining the Club

I joined the Calgary Section of the Alpine Club of Canada in 1968 and did a couple of climbs with them and took one of their mountaineering courses, but I let that membership lapse after a couple of years. Then in 1977 I joined the main club and have been a member ever since. I still use the backcountry huts and volunteer for different things.

In 1978 Flo Smith, Jan Boschman and I skied into the Alpine Club's Wates-Gibson Hut in the Tonquin Valley in Jasper National Park. The weather was totally socked in so we saw nothing except for a tiny bit of Surprise Peak for five out of six days. The last night we stayed at the Edith Cavell Hostel and woke up to brilliant sunshine! Because of this we went back the next year and had good weather and great skiing.

Three Damsels

The clouds were hanging low over the mountains when Jan Boschman and I left the University of Calgary's Kananaskis field station at Barrier Lake and headed towards the Tonquin Valley in Jasper National Park. Jan left in her truck at 7:45 a.m., but I got held up waiting for Kelly, my dog, to come home. Silver had taken him off hunting as usual. While pacing the floor waiting I managed to get my truck started, warmed up, the apartment vacuumed, and a cup of tea consumed. At long last—it seemed an eternity—and with Peter Jonker's help, Kelly showed up and we took off for the great adventure.

Heading north from Lake Louise the highway became icy and the clouds looked ominous. Creeping up Sunwapta Pass towards the Columbia Icefield it was snowing heavily, which dampened my spirits rapidly. Across from Hilda Creek hostel Jan waved me down and informed me that the center linkage on her truck had been bent when she skidded and hit a snow bank. She had ingeniously straightened it out with her jack, so she was able to carefully drive into Jasper with me close behind.

In Jasper we left her truck at a garage and piled all her gear into mine and headed for the Edith Cavell Road. On our way north we had stopped and informed the rest of our party of our problems, so they had started up the trail ahead of us.

Donning our packs (Kelly included) at the Edith Cavell Road (which is closed in winter) we made good time on the 8-mile ski trip to the Edith Cavell Hostel. About a quarter mile before the hostel we passed Rich Kroeker and his friend Ron, the hardier members of our party, filling their faces to enable them to make the last quarter mile. Flo Smith and Ed Kroeker met us as we reached the hostel. They were brandishing cups of coffee in their hands, but had no tea for us.

All six of us crashed in the girls' dorm, got a fire lit and ate the concoction that Flo and Ed brewed for our supper. Another party of six people was in the boys' dorm.

Sunday morning we dragged our butts out of the sleeping bags and downed some breakfast, then, laced with numerous cups of tea, we skied off down the trail towards the Tonquin Valley. Ron got side tracked at Cavell Lake, a quarter mile down the trail, with a bad case of blisters and lethargy. The old lady of the group charged on ahead leaving everyone else behind. After a mile or so Ed decided to turn back so sent Rich in hot pursuit of the old lady to make her wait for a picture taking spree. In due course the spree occurred and then Jan, Flo, and I took off to the Tonquin Valley, while Rich, Ron, and Ed headed back to civilization and mundane things called work.

The snow was sticky but with a well-beaten track the going was easy and the sun was out. Eleven miles later we arrived at the Wates-Gibson Hut at Outpost Lake at 5 p.m. and were soon downing lots of hot tea and chatting with Brian and Bill who were working on insulating part of the hut. The hut was housing a number of people and others arrived off and on during our stay. No one except Bill left before we did.

On the Monday we teamed up with two gals from Golden and Vancouver and skied over to Amethyst Lake via a hairy bushwhacking route led by the old lady. At the lake we succumbed to temptation and lay in the sun, sipping more tea and filling ourselves with the goodies we had brought along. We'll do anything to lighten our packs.

That evening we had a rousing game of *Hearts* while huddled in our duvet jackets in the cold hut. I kept falling asleep between turns and had to be wakened to play my hand. Once I stammered out the words, "Oh, is it my serve?"

On Tuesday, the old lady once more led the parade of five girls up the Eremite Valley. She very cleverly maneuvered two strong girls into the trail breaking position with directive comments now and then. We had lunch at the top of a lovely little ridge wrapped in our duvet jackets as the sun was not entirely obliging. The view of the Eremite Glacier was superb—it felt like we could almost touch it. At the bottom of a possibly dangerous slope we turned back for a marvellous downhill powder ski. After amusing ourselves at a snow-covered waterfall the old lady turned back towards the hut with her dog in tow, supposedly to put the kettle on, but on the flats below the hut she was sidetracked by the sun and the view of Fraser Glacier.

That evening we had a quieter game of *Oh Hell*. I was winning quite nicely until I started sleeping between turns again.

The highlight day of the trip was on Wednesday when we once more skied to Amethyst Lake and to tree line on Clitheroe Meadows. Sitting in the sun under a perfectly blue sky and gradually burning to a crisp, again lightening our packs of goodies. After lunch the old lady got inspired and climbed up the ridge between Mounts Clitheroe and Old Horn with Flo, Jan, and Kelly in pursuit. When the old lady was almost at the top of the ridge Jan admitted to being scared and Flo to being dehydrated so we turned back and made multiple tracks in the snow down the steep slope, and took what are, hopefully, impressive photos.

The view from Clitheroe Meadows on a clear blue-sky day is nothing less than spectacular, marvellous, and glorious. Mountains, well over 10,000 and 11,000 feet studded with gleaming glaciers everywhere. The biggest cathedral I have ever been in.

The ski down from the meadows was fantastic, with lots of room for turns and adventure. Jan was heard to say that all trees should be that far apart.

We were rather late getting back to the hut even though we found a better bushwhacking route around Surprise Point.

Thursday was leaving day—sad, but glorious. We packed up what little food we had left (in spite of our best efforts we did not get it all eaten) and skied down the trail to the Astoria River and civilization. Eighteen miles in one day.

Skiing Adventures

Following these adventures, I somehow got hooked up with George Stefanick's week-long ski camps in the Tonquin Valley staying in the Wates-Gibson Hut. I attended ten of his camps. During part of that time I was struggling with intestinal problems and finding it difficult to stick to a restricted diet at the camps. I also wanted to go to some different places while I was still strong enough to deal with the ski terrain, so I volunteered to run ski camps for the Rocky Mountain Section of the Club.

To be sure I wasn't eating foods that made me sick I would precook the meats and desserts and freeze them in tinfoil trays. This turned out to be a blessing as all we had to do at the camp was to thaw the frozen food, use frozen vegetables and make a carbohydrate. It eased the burden of food preparation at the hut. Chuck O'Callaghan loved it and always raved about my meals. Roast turkey in gravy was a big hit.

Through the years I ran ski camps in Rogers Pass in the Selkirk Mountains (with Lloyd 'Kiwi' Gallagher as guide), Monashee Chalet in the Monashee mountains, the Clemenceau Icefield, and Dave Henry Lodge in the Selwyn range. I also went with the Edmonton Section on ski camps to the Freshfield Icefield, Kokanee Glacier Provincial Park, and Fairy Meadow in the Adamant Range. In 1983 I attended a camp at Rogers Pass and 24 years later Jane Steed, who had been the cook, recognized me at a Banff Mountain Book Festival!

The Freshfield Icefield is the most beautiful place I've ever been in the winter and the Clemenceau Icefield is the second. Of course, the Wapta Icefield, that I have skied several times, probably comes in third for spectacular scenery.

I also participated in a number of fall hiking camps that the Edmonton section organized, in places such as Rogers Pass and Waterton Lakes National Park. This section of the club had some older members who enjoyed these camps. Going on these week long camps enabled me to see a lot of beautiful mountains, that I would not have seen otherwise, and meet many wonderful people.

Mount Assiniboine Ski Camp

"I'm going to Mount Assiniboine, I'm going to Mount Assiniboine," I sang and danced gaily around my little house. I had just received a phone call from the Alpine Club that they could use me as cook at their 1981 Mount Assiniboine ski camp and I was deliriously happy.

I had always wanted to go to Mount Assiniboine in the winter, but it was a two-day ski trip into the mountain with at least one very dangerous avalanche slope to ski down. Recently I wanted to go in order to further my research for a biography I was writing about Lizzie Rummel. Now, not only was I getting the chance to go, but also a free helicopter flight into the mountain, time to ski, time to do research—and I would get paid for cooking as well. I was in seventh heaven.

The day arrived. I had a truckload of groceries for thirteen people for eight days and I was sitting at the Banff heliport waiting for the helicopter. Mount Assiniboine is 35.4 aerial miles (59 km) over the Alberta boundary from the Town of Banff in British

Columbia. The mountain itself is 11,870 feet (3618 metres) high and very similar to the Matterhorn in Switzerland. The area receives a vast amount of snow that lasts well into late spring and summer. I had often hiked into the mountain in the summer but it had never worked out as a winter trip.

As I sat in my truck at the heliport I fretted because the helicopter was late in arriving. "Whatever could be keeping him?" Soon I found out that an accident victim had been taken to Calgary 74 miles (123 km) away. The chopper arrived back at the heliport two hours late, but I really didn't mind.

We were off. Rising quickly from the Bow Valley floor we headed up the Brewster Creek Valley. The view was fantastic. Mountains everywhere, snow and evergreen trees by the acre. The scene was unbelievably beautiful. Soon we were passing the skiers who the pilot was to pick up after dropping me off. They had skied to Quartz Ridge from the Sunshine ski resort. We waved gaily as we flew over so they would know they had not been forgotten.

As we flew over the Valley of the Rocks we could see Mount Assiniboine shining in the sun and rising fifteen hundred feet above the surrounding peaks. It was a perfect blue-sky day. Soon Assiniboine Lodge came into view and we landed in front of it. There was a great cluster of people standing by the lodge waiting to be flown out to Quartz Ridge. Quick hands unloaded the food boxes for my ski party and then four people jumped into the chopper and were off to Quartz Ridge.

While I moved the food from the landing site into the lodge the pilot moved the outgoing party to Quartz Ridge and brought the Alpine Club party into the lodge four at a time. Soon our ten skiers had all arrived and the others had all gone, so we sat down to tea in the dining room.

While we sipped tea from great steaming mugs Ky, the lodge manager, gave a small talk on the routine of the lodge and then wished us all happy skiing.

As the members of the party hauled their packs to their rooms and got settled in, I cooked dinner. Later we all got acquainted around the fire. It would be hard to find a more interesting group of people. From university professor to retired teacher of the deaf, each person became a story that everyone was anxious to hear. It was one of those times when everyone's personality meshed well.

Each day the ten skiers would go skiing with their lunch, which was made the night before, stuffed in their pack along with other gear and I would cook or ski as time permitted. The first day, of course, was the best weather and I felt I should stay in the kitchen and work hard so I could ski with the group the whole of the second day. The day was broken up, however, with visitors from the Naiset huts a kilometre away and Ky's Norwegian wife Eva also kept me entertained with stories of Norway. I was avidly interested in Norway as my grandparents had emigrated from there, but I had never known them.

One day Margaret and I skied over to Lizzie Rummel's old cabin, which was about two kilometres away over many little hills. Using the key that Ky loaned me, I went inside and visualized Lizzie in this setting where she had spent twenty years. Shivering in the cold, dark cabin I regaled Margaret with stories of Lizzie and her prowess in the mountains. A truly remarkable woman, but that is another story in another place.

There were days the snow was great and days when it got very soft. It was early

53

May and the weather was very warm. One night it rained and the snow became quite rotten. When we arrived the snow had been about seven feet deep around the lodge, but as the weather continued to be warm we soon found ourselves sinking to the tops of our legs if we didn't wear our skis to go to the outhouse. Even the cook's outhouse, which was close to the lodge, was an adventure to reach when the snow was melting. This outhouse had one of the most beautiful views imaginable from its door. We usually kept the door open all the time as one could not be seen from the lodge and it was great seeing Naiset Peak from its perch.

The best snow was usually in the morning, so one morning I went to Wonder Pass by myself. I had bread or pies to make in the afternoon so could not go for the day with the group. I enjoy skiing alone as there is plenty of time to commune with God while surrounded by the beautiful mountains. One could see for miles from the top of Wonder Pass. It was with great reluctance that I left the pass and skied back to the lodge. The downhill skiing was fantastic—beautiful powder snow on a good solid base. I made some of my best turns on that ski trip.

Eremite/Tonquin Ski Camp

Published in The Breeze an Alpine Club of Canada section newsletter 1985.

This ski camp came into being under the terrific organization and leadership of George Stefanick. George has long had a concern for older members of the ACC and has been organizing camps for them in recent years. This camp was largely made up of retired people with a few younger ones thrown in for good measure. George's daughter Lorna was the youngest participant at age 24 and Dr. Morley Tuttle the oldest at age 74, a fifty-year age range. In spite of the age range the younger members of the party did not show any resentment when the older participants left them panting and gasping on the slopes!

The group consisted of twenty participants of all shapes and sizes. Ruth Robinson, a New York Times editor (New York), was ecstatic to finally see the Ramparts in living colour after looking at Travel Alberta literature photos for years. Peggy Bussell (West Vancouver) had cycled and hiked in the Rockies in 1945 (Little Yoho with Ken Jones) and had met her tall, lanky husband, Jack, through the ACC some thirty years ago. Bob Twiss (Edmonton) tried valiantly to wear out Bob Nicholl (Edmonton), twenty-five years his junior, on the telemarking slopes of Surprise Point and almost made it. Fred Narten (Edmonton) did marvellously well on the woodpile (as did others) and kept up with the other grey hairs on the trail. Margaret McDonald (Edmonton), a retired social worker of almost 70 years, was pretty nimble on her skis and didn't slow down during Happy Hour either. Mary and Howard Rode (North Vancouver) cut some pretty impressive curves on the Penstock Creek slopes and kept some fine fires burning in the hut. Paul and Beverley Kebarle (Edmonton) kept up with the best of the skiers and Paul, a brilliant chemist, caught onto the UNO game pretty fast, while Bev knew every word of every song that was sung. Jim Race (Edmonton) was found constantly by Lorna's side and vice versa. Between them they make a mean chili and Lorna is very good at holding up hut posts at six in the morning after the night before. Ken Parley (Burnaby), a retired science teacher and his vivacious wife Shirley were great at getting lost the first day and turned out to be enthusiastic UNO players. Jim Unsworth (Edmonton) slogged along with the stronger skiers, although he lost interest in George's trip to Thunderbolt Pass due to crust and wind. Jim skied out alone on the Friday to meet his wife, Judy, who was too essential to Canada Post for them to let her come on the trip. On the Friday Ruthie Oltmann (Exshaw) took a cleaning fit and scrubbed toilets and kitchen shelves. The disease spread rapidly to Bob Nicholl and George, so in an afternoon the kitchen became spotless. Morley Tuttle became known for his arduous trips such as *Morley's Revenge* on Surprise Point and for exhausting some of the participants to the point where they had to have a day of rest after a trip with him. George Stefanick, a retired engineer, was no slouch on the slopes and left some of the younger members behind as he plodded towards Thunderbolt Pass and skied eight out of eight days.

All members of the party contributed to cooking the marvellous meals,

Dennis Utterback, guide Paul Mesorobian, John Christian and Ruthie, on an unnamed peak in the Wapta Icefield, 1989.

washing up, wood chopping, water hauling and lamp lighting under George's very fair duty roster.

The Dixons, who have a camp on Amethyst Lake, hauled all the gear and food into the hut by skidoo and also took the participants up the Edith Cavell Road to the youth hostel from whence they skied the 18 kilometres to the hut. During the camp, trips were made up the Eremite Valley, across Amethyst Lake to Dixons' camp, to Moat Lake and Vista Pass, Clitheroe Meadows, Surprise Point telemarking slopes, and to slopes on Outpost Peak near the hut.

For the trip out on the last day, the party split up and half the group skied out the Astoria River/Edith Cavell Road (30 km), while the other half skied out Maccarib Pass/Portal Creek (34 km). Four of the latter group were over 65 years of age, including Morley at 74 years.

During the camp excellent snow conditions were encountered as well as very crusty and windy conditions. Overall the skiing was super and everyone had a wonderful holiday. George's excellent organization of the camp was greatly appreciated and everyone asked to be put on his mailing list. While the camp was largely for retired members, it was agreed that having younger people along was a good safety feature as they would have the youth and brawn to ski out in a hurry should an emergency arise. The fifty-year range in ages made the socializing more interesting and more revealing. Some people didn't need youth on their side to enjoy Happy Hour!

Freshfield Ski Camp

The Freshfield ski camp in Banff National Park 1987 was made up of eleven participants from Maryland, U.S.A., Edmonton, Kamloops, Prince George, Canmore and Exshaw, with an average age of 48 years. It was one of those fantastic camps where the first seven out of eight days had perfect, sunny weather. This created a good market for glacier cream, which prevented blisters, but not fabulous tans.

Getting there was half the fun. At first it was following various people in their cars, supposedly knowing where they were going, up a series of gravel roads in the Blaeberry Valley north of Golden, then back down them again, and on up another wild goose chase, which finally resulted in reaching the helicopter staging site. The flight up the Blaeberry Valley and over the Mummery Group was a bit of heaven as the weather was clear and sunny. On the B.C./Alberta boundary where the party landed (2825 m), there was a very cold wind, but once down off the Helmer/Gilgit Col it was warm and wonderful. It took five hours to ski to the Lloyd Mackay Hut with the party on four ropes.

During the week, ascents were made of the ridge of Mount Niverville, up the Niverville Glacier twice to three different cols, the summit of Mount Gilgit, a col beside the northeast face of Mount Freshfield, and a col on the Pangman Glacier. Short excursions were also made in the treed area above the hut to overlook the Pangman Glacier and the lake below the Freshfield Glacier.

The Lloyd Mackay Hut proved to be sufficiently warm due to its high level of insulation, solar heat and twelve bodies. In fact, the door had to be kept open to relieve

Mount Freshfield, 1987.

stuffiness. This also meant that the local pack rat had to be chased out of the food kept in the hut. Graham Walker spent hours on the pack rat patrol during the night and subsequently hours recovering during the day. A ptarmigan was sighted one day and heard clucking during the night.

Jutta Seehafer was camp manager and George Stefanick did his best to keep the party organized in the hut. His 6:30 a.m. breakfasts were always appreciated, but not always the early hour. Neil Lauzon, the huts maintenance man, cleaned the hut, put up curtains, added covers to the foamies, and cleaned out the biffy. This latter project required a crowbar and climbing ropes. The ropes were to hold the biffy from flying down to the Freshfield glacier during the cleaning operation.

The route out on the last day was down the Freshfield Glacier, across the lake (which had formed in the last fifty years), bushwhacking for hours down Freshfield Creek and various escapades across the flats where Freshfield Greek, Forbes Greek and the Howse River join, before ascending for the helicopter pick up.

A super-marvellous week.

The Nightmare

It was another Alpine Club ski camp at the Wates-Gibson Hut in the Tonquin Valley of Jasper National Park. Sleeping accommodation in Canada's alpine huts is communal and this hut has a loft with sleeping platforms. One just lays out their sleeping bag where they find a spot—like sausages in a pan. My spot was with Krystyna Jahns on one side and Sandy Anderson on the other. We weren't crowded, so it was nice and roomy.

One night I was dreaming that it was summertime at this hut and was going to the biffy in the night. Most of us get up for these nocturnal trips. It was dark and the route was by the front of the hut and then through a dark copse of trees just before the biffy. In my dream I was thinking that someone might jump out of the dark copse of trees and grab me, so when I reached that point in my dream I started yelling. Only I was yelling in real life, not just in the dream. But I was still sleeping. Sandy rolled over and grabbed me by the shoulders to wake me up and I thought it was the person in my dream, so I yelled louder! He shook me harder and finally woke me up. I muttered something about dreaming and promptly fell back to sleep. However, twenty people in the hut were now wide-awake! They gradually traipsed out to the biffy one by one while I slept on. In the morning I apologized profusely to everyone and every last one of them said, "Don't worry, we had to go out anyway."

The Birthday Party

The Alpine Club of Canada's Wheeler Hut is in Rogers Pass, British Columbia, part of Glacier National Park. It is extremely popular in winter for ski mountaineering.

In 1998 I was running a week-long ski camp for the Rocky Mountain Section of the Club. Val Sullivan was having a birthday in the middle of the week, so I had made little notes for everyone and put them in envelopes I had made from used calendar pictures. In each envelope was a note about a surprise party for Val and I asked each person to dream up some kind of a gift like a poem or song, or whatever. Val's envelope, of course, said something different. No one was to reveal what was in his or her envelope.

A couple of nights before the party we were all sleeping in the loft when a puff of wind off the glacier blew the screen in the window onto the floor with a crash. I woke up screaming in one end of the loft and Val woke up yelling "Fire, fire" in the other end.

The night of the birthday party arrived. I had fancy birthday tablecloths, cake plates and glasses all to match and a birthday cake with candles—a festive affair. After dinner everyone gave Val gifts. The five guys from Utah sang a song that Edgar Webster had composed that was very funny. The two Irish guys, Chuck O'Callaghan and Bill Hanlon, lustily sang Irish songs and Dave Smith gave Val a big brown paper bag and inside it was a fire extinguisher!

Val said it was the best birthday party she'd ever had.

Tonquin Valley Ski Camp

Email to: "Ingrid & Stu Cummings"
Thanks for the photos and the announcements about the arrival of yet more grandchildren. I'm glad everyone is doing well. The church ladies sound wonderful. My 2003 Tonquin Valley Ski camp was great. Two days to ski into

the hut, staying at the Edith Cavell Hostel on the way. It was very cold for the first three days, but it warmed up. The second day it took me three hours to warm up my right toes—it took that long to get to the sun—but they were not frozen, just cold. I keep wiggling them. For some reason my right foot toes get cold really easily. I think it's related to my lower back that is getting old and decrepit. I celebrated my 66th birthday by skiing with the group on the Surprise Point slopes. Properly shredded by us all. Calf-deep powder snow. The night before my birthday Lucille made two birthday cakes (to feed 15 people) with six candles on each! She forgot the balloons she'd brought until the last night, but put them up that night.

One day I had an easy morning, and then did ten laps around Outpost Lake (where the hut is situated)—two hours. It's not a big lake. There wasn't the usual amount of snow, but adequate and good quality. I had a *Ruthie Rant* one day. Stan Rosenbaum wanted to clear Ada's Boulevard, a route that is a short cut across to Amethyst Lake so we wouldn't have so much difficulty bushwhacking. Krystyna Jahns and I followed him and then I left him to his explorations and continued on the already packed route. On the way back, later in the day, we were together and I started out helping him, gave up and followed the already packed route, and then tried following other tracks (supposedly on Ada's Blvd.) further along. Had an awful time and was muttering invectives at Ada when I heard voices above. There were some others of the group returning with Stan in tow, so I got up to them with much ranting and raving about stupid Ada, and why did someone always want to find the proper Ada's Blvd? I got teased for the rest of the day about *Ruthie's Rant*. I shall never again follow someone who thinks they can find the true Ada's Blvd. This happens every year I've been there. Elusive Ada is just that, elusive. It's best to just break a bushwhack trail and keep to it instead of wandering all through the forest looking for elusive Ada.

So, sister Ingrid, no one left me anywhere. In fact, one day when we skied over to Clitheroe Meadows to the warden's cabin I wanted to go higher on the mountain, but three people wanted to go back to the hut, so I consented to lead them via the "summer trail". I'd done it by myself the day before. We took it and I was leading, thus setting the pace (slow, but steady) on the more level sections; Sandy and Lorraine Anderson were absolutely thrilled with my leadership pace and the things I taught them by just doing it such as regrouping every once in awhile and I don't know what else. They were so ecstatic that they went on and on about it and both gave me a big hug. That made me feel like I'd had a mission.

There, you now have another story.

Happy trails,

—Ruthie

National Parks Centennial

Published in the Banff Crag & Canyon newspaper in 1985

Hikers standing on the moraine below Mt. Victoria recently watched a long line of ants crawling down the lower Victoria Glacier. The long line of ants turned out to be twenty-seven members of the Alpine Club of Canada descending from Abbot Pass (2926 m) on the second leg of an historic hike organized to mark the National Parks Centennial year which is being celebrated across Canada in all national parks.

The party of climbers and hikers commenced their journey on July 27, 1985 at the Lake O'Hara gate near Wapta Lake in Yoho National Park. From this point they were bussed into the Lake O'Hara Lodge where they were served coffee on the verandah of the lodge. It is unusual for large parties to be allowed to hike in the Lake O'Hara region due to its delicate alpine nature. Because of the historic nature of this trek, however, the Yoho National Park officials made an exception to the rule and they are to be congratulated on their efficient handling of the situation. Four alpine guides were present to add credence to the part the Swiss guides played in opening up the Canadian Rockies to climbing. The four guides, Peter Fuhrmann, Bernie Schiesser, Eric Lomas and Ernst Salzgeber split the group into three parties and led them from the lodge to Lake Oesa and Abbot Pass. Yoho National Park wardens met the party at the Lake O'Hara Lodge and Lake Oesa. Mike, the park warden who accompanied the group up the long scree climb to the pass, took the National Parks Centennial Flag with him and many pictures were taken in front of the hut with the flag to mark the historic trek.

Abbot Pass itself has a unique history, so it was fitting the Alpine Club chose to re-enact the ascent of Abbot Pass made in 1896 by Philip Abbot after whom the pass was named. Abbot was a member of the American Appalachian Mountain Club and was climbing Mount Lefroy on the south side of the pass when he fell to his death. Abbot Pass Hut was also named after Philip Abbot and stands as a memorial to the Swiss guides who built it in 1922 under the auspices of the Canadian Pacific Railway. In this era before helicopters ingenious methods had to be used to erect a building at 2926 metres. The main structure of the hut is rock from the surroundings, but the timbers had to be brought from Lake Louise. Horses hauled them to the base of the glacier and from there they were winched up the glacier to the pass. The winch was set up on the pass and one man acted as a counterweight to haul them. For sixty years this hut stood as the highest placed building in Canada, then in 1982 the Neil Colgan Hut was built on the shoulder of Mount Little in the Valley of Ten Peaks and is now the highest placed building at 2940 metres.

For this National Parks Centennial trek the Abbot Pass Hut acted as the overnight stop for the participants. Many of the party did not know each other prior to the hike and the wide range of ages was a testimony to the fact that where mountains are concerned there is no generation gap. Henry Ness, at 77 years, was the oldest in the party and his 13 year old granddaughter, Susan, was the youngest.

The idea for the Alpine Club to do something to mark the National Parks Centennial came from the Banff/Lake Louise Chamber of Commerce, and Eric Lomas' organization, with cooperation and guidance from the Yoho National Park officials, brought this historic trek into being. The importance of the event and the concern for the delicate nature of the Lake O'Hara region was evident in that several of the club's board members were on the hike. Peter Fuhrmann, club president, Jim Murphy, clubhouse chairman, Bernie Schiesser, huts committee chairman, Eric Lomas, chairman of the Banff Section of the Club and Ernst Salzgeber, vice-chairman.

Since the Alpine Club is basically a climbing club two alpine ascents were made. Jim Murphy and Ernst Salzgeber climbed Mount Lefroy (3423 m) on the Saturday and about two-thirds of the party climbed the south peak of Mt. Victoria (3464 m) on the Sunday which included Deanne Fuhrmann and Susan Ness both thirteen years old. The whole party roped up for the descent down The Death Trap of the lower Victoria Glacier at noon on the Sunday and formed the long line of ants the hikers on the moraine below could see. Due to the recent warm weather, the snow on the glaciers had largely melted and the route down was one of the safest in history, particularly for such a large party. Two of the hut custodians also joined for the descent to Lake Louise, thus making up the twenty-seven members.

After unroping at the base of the glacier the group hiked to the Plain of Six Glaciers Teahouse and promptly ate all the blueberry and apple pie in sight. The hike continued from the teahouse to the Lake Louise parking lot where tourists from around the world uttered words of congratulations.

While most members of the party had been on glaciers before, some had not. One gentleman said if he had known what the expedition involved he would never have chosen to go, but realized when it was finished he would not have missed it for the world! The weather was superb, the views of mountains and glaciers were fantastic and the company was excellent. It was a memorable and exciting event.

Mount Athabasca

At one time Charlie Locke owned seven downhill ski resorts, but long before he became famous for that he had a mountain guide's license and was a prolific climber doing many first ascents. In 1968 he taught the Calgary hostel group's snow and ice school at the Columbia Icefield in Jasper National Park. The first day we practiced cutting steps in the Athabasca Glacier and doing crevasse rescue. The second day we climbed Mount Athabasca.

Thirty years later the Alpine Club was celebrating the centennial of the first ascent of Mount Athabasca that happened in 1898. I managed to get on the climb by writing the following article.

The Thirty-Year Itch

Article published by Mountain Heritage Magazine—Autumn 1998

Goals! Some of us set them and some just drift along. I am a goal setter, but I've had my drifting moments. Thirty years ago I was an active member of what was then called the Canadian Hostelling Association and I drifted along with the activities of the outdoors side of the club. Thus, I became involved in a snow and ice school taught by the guide Charlie Locke, on the Athabasca Glacier, which resulted in a climb of Mount Athabasca.

Recollecting my ascent of the mountain on July 7, 1968 is not hard. I have the facility of a good memory when it comes to my mountain activities. I recall walking up the glacier and then later looking down and seeing an avalanche had fallen very close to our tracks. On the top of the first peak my friend and fellow climber Mary Campbell didn't feel like going further. I think she was just tired. I stayed with her and so I didn't make the summit. We sat there and enjoyed the spectacular view, but also thought about Mig Morton, who had died in an avalanche on nearby Parker Ridge the previous December. It was a sad time as well as a marvellous time.

I was disappointed not to make the summit of Mount Athabasca. Even though Mary insisted I go on, I wasn't the kind of person to leave someone alone on a mountain. Mary is a good friend and it didn't seem right to leave her there; it just isn't good mountaineering practice, and I guess I'm just not a peak bagger. A peak bagger is someone who will push for the top no matter what the risks. I've missed a few summits over the years because I was not a peak bagger. Sometimes I wish I were. I regret not going further on several occasions.

These days I try harder to get to the summit, even if it's only a scramble. Sometimes we all fall short of our goals but now I like to think of myself as a finisher. Finishers like to complete a project, whether it be climbing a mountain or writing a book. I guess that has something to do with my desire to get to the top of mountains.

Mount Athabasca once more looms large on my horizon. This year is not only the 100th anniversary of the first ascent of the mountain by Norman Collie and Herman Woolley – it is also the thirtieth anniversary of my own first attempt. The 100th anniversary celebrations are scheduled for August 18th and 19th and will include a centennial climb of Mount Athabasca. Special flags will be placed on the summit and there is a desire to return the first climbers' ice axe as well. Personally, I'm planning on taking my wood handled ice axe, which I used during my climb of 1968.

Shortly after I heard about the centennial climb my sense of adventure took hold of me. I wanted to be there. Maybe there's something of a peak bagger in me after all. I don't want to lose my compassion, but I do want to make it to the summit this time. It's not that life will be over if I don't make it, but when I pass the spot where Mary and I stopped, I know I'm going to be exhilarated. I'll finally finish a climb I started thirty years ago.

Mount Athabasca 1998

The Centennial of the first ascent of Mount Athabasca took place in 1998 and the Alpine Club of Canada, together with Parks Canada, celebrated with a Centennial ascent of the mountain and a dedication to A.O. Wheeler who had done the boundary survey along the Great Divide of the mountains. Doing the centennial climb appealed to me because it was 30 years since I first climbed it and I thought I could do it. I approached Bob Sandford, the organizer, and managed to get on the climb through writing the foregoing article.

There were a lot of festivities prior to and after the climb. The night before the twenty-seven climbers had a meeting and it was decided that no matter where we were on the mountain the next day at 11:00 a.m. everyone would turn back. It was at this hour that the Wheeler dedication was to take place at the Icefield Centre. I was on a rope with Lisa Paulson leading and Leslie Jaquette. We were approaching the top of the Silverhorn (my high point in 1968) when the 11:00 o'clock hour came over Lisa's radio. We looked at each other and Lisa said, "Do you want to turn around?" Leslie and I both said, "No way." On we went and got to the summit in a total whiteout. We ignored the previous day's commitment because we were so close to the summit.

It took us eight hours to get to the top because a couple of days before the climb I had sprained my big toe, and was taking Tylenol every four hours, which slowed me down. I had deliberately not told anyone about the problem toe because I thought they wouldn't let me go. It took almost thirteen hours for the whole climb. Afterwards we rushed to Jasper for showers and the Jasper Park Lodge celebration dinner. At one point during the dinner, Leslie and I looked at each other and burst into laughter. We were both so tired we looked bushed. In spite of being totally exhausted it was an exciting experience, and in spite of my sprained toe and my sixty-one years I was thrilled to make it to the summit at last.

More Articles in Club Publications

Herbert Markus Kaufman

(Obituary published in the 1995 Canadian Alpine Journal)
Born April 25, 1944, in Altshausen, Germany. Herbert Kaufman passed away on December 16, 1994, at home after a strong battle with leukemia. Herb is survived by his loving friend, Carole Kirk, his children, Christa, Petra, and Ian, his mother, Klara, his brother, Paul, and many relatives in Germany. He was a trained pastry chef and spent two years in Switzerland and three years in England before coming to Canada in 1967. In 1974 Herb bought Pop's Bakery in Banff, and later he took over the Bread Basket in Canmore.

Herb was an active member of St. Mary's Catholic Church, the Rotary Club, and the community, especially as a ballroom dancer. He will be remembered in the Bow Valley for his love of the mountains, skiing, hiking, jogging and curling.

Herb was a Rocky Mountain Section member of the Alpine Club of Canada who lived in Banff. I first met him when he came on our Monashee Chalet ski camp in 1992 that I organized. At that time, I gave him a lift to Blue River the day before the camp and during our ride I learned a lot about the bakery business. He definitely was a very committed baker. This later showed up in the camp when he couldn't keep his hands out of the baking business and proceeded to make us scones from whatever ingredients he could find. (We already had dozens of his whole wheat buns that I had bought from his Bread Basket store.) Herb also attended our Dave Henry Lodge ski camp (1993) and the Eremite-Tonquin Valley ski camp at the Wates-Gibson Hut (1994). He was an enthusiastic participant at the ski camps, both in skiing and in making scones or buns from pancake mix. After he attended the Monashee camp, he convinced several of his friends to attend the next two camps, and we all benefited from meeting these wonderful people. I know they will miss him very much.

Words cannot convey a person's personality. When I think of Herb, I can hear his clipped speech, and see his eyebrows flicking as he talked, and his tousled head as he came into the hut kitchen in the mornings. His big grin and great enthusiasm for the ski camps will be missed.

I was all set to throw in an extra bag of pancake mix in the food supplies for all my ski camps in the future because Herb was planning on attending them all. Now I won't have to do that, and I really wish this wasn't so.

We'll miss you Herb. Adieu.

—Ruthie

But it Was Fun … Mostly

Article published in the January 2006 issue of The Blizzard. The newsletter of the Rocky Mountain Section of the Alpine Club of Canada.

Do you remember what a Gestetner is? If you don't have any idea then you are showing your youth! A Gestetner is a copying machine that drove a lot of people up the wall, including me. First you typed your information on this long, strange looking sheet and if you made a mistake you dabbed a bit of red stuff on the wrong letters, waited for it to dry and typed the right letters on top of the red stuff. Your finished product usually had a lot of red spots on it. Then you attached the holes at the top of the sheet to the Gestetner machine and hand cranked it to see what a finished copy would look like. If it was okay you started the motor of the machine and away it went, running off the number of copies you required. Invariably the machine would have a hitch and have to be stopped. I usually lost some of my hair at this point – from pulling it out in frustration! Denis DeMontigny, the Clubhouse custodian at the time, frequently saved my neck with that infernal machine. That was how I got my first *Blizzards* copied in the early to mid 1980s.

Then came photocopiers. First I would type up the *Blizzard* on my little portable typewriter, then I would add some calligraphy that everyone thought was beautiful. Finally I would run it off on a photocopier. Needless to say, we didn't have 700 plus members at the time. These photocopied *Blizzards* were an improvement over the Gestetner issues, but now as I look back at a 1989 issue, it doesn't look as good as it did back then.

The next improvement came when Roger Peterson, an ACC member from Boulder, Colorado, volunteered to do the layout for the *Blizzard*. I would type all the articles and ads and mail them to him. He would then do the layout (he is a whiz with computers) and "fast mail" the print-ready *Blizzard* back to me. That was how the *Blizzard* was prepared from 1989 to 1992.

Some time in 1992 I bought a Mac computer and Roger came all the way from Boulder to help me take over the graphics and layout. Of course, not only was I learning how to use a computer, I was also learning the most difficult desktop publishing program there was at the time—QuarkXPress. I had a lot of help during this period from people like Craig Linnen, Bev Bendell and Eileen Phillips, who did the *Blizzard* for a year when I stress-fractured my hip.

Stuffing the *Blizzard* into envelopes became one of my jobs during this period, and I had a dedicated group of volunteers to help me out. At one point Kathy Punshon followed by Gary Brown became stuffing coordinators and relieved me of that job. However, when Gary resigned, I took over the stuffing coordination once again. Finally this past year the *Blizzard* stuffing became too much for me. Hauling boxes of *Blizzards* up and down stairs and in and out of buildings, and doing the whole job alone at least twice was overwhelming. It was a great relief when the R.M.S. executive agreed that I could outsource the stuffing and mailing to a local business. It felt like magic!

A few weeks ago, at the November 2005 AGM, I mentioned that I was going to retire from the editorship in another year. Forewarned is forearmed was my idea! Later Doug Fulford spoke to me about doing it and after a meeting at my house in front of the computer he volunteered to become the editor.

Welcome to the job, Doug. I wish you all the best.

New Editor: The Rocky Mountain Section expresses its sincere thanks to Ruthie Oltmann for her tireless efforts over the last 17 years.

Rockies Gal Visits Bon Echo

Published in the Alpine Club of Canada's "Gazette" Summer 2007

What's a Rockies gal doing in Ontario anyhow? Well, actually, she was attending family events and visiting relatives and friends at the leisurely pace of two months. Since she was driving and camping it was a good opportunity to assuage her curiosity and check out a hut that isn't in the mountains.

Fortunately it pays to be the ACC librarian because you end up connecting with people you might not know otherwise. One of those people was David Brown who had contacted me about putting copies of the new Bon Echo guidebook into the ACC library and Clubhouse. In our email messages I told him I was interested in visiting Bon Echo Hut while in Ontario in the fall. He very kindly emailed me a couple of maps and through emails I met Geoff Hodgson, the hut custodian for the weekend I wished to visit, and thus the stage was set to see a hut outside of the mountains.

Bon Echo Hut is situated just outside Bon Echo Provincial Park which is located between Toronto and Ottawa on Highway 41, 30 km north of Highway 7 and has a landscape dominated by one of the most imposing natural phenomena in Ontario—Mazinaw Rock. The granite cliffs rise majestically out of Mazinaw Lake, providing a very impressive focal point in the park and have been dubbed "the Canadian Gibraltar." They are about 100 metres high, about 2 km long and are home to more than 120 climbing routes from 5.0 to 5.12.

The provincial park is situated on the edge of Mazinaw Lake, which is 13 km long, up to 2 km wide and 120 metres deep and is divided into two halves by a spit of land. The narrow point dividing the lake is only 10 metres wide and has occasionally been waded by climbers with their packs held high above their heads. The park campground is on the west side of the lake and the cliffs and hut are on the east side.

I arrived and camped at Bon Echo Provincial Park the night before I was to meet Geoff and was able to check my email at the Town of Cloyne south of the park for the first time since leaving home a month earlier. Fortunately I found a message from Geoff with his cell phone number. Previously I'd arranged to meet him at the public dock on Mazinaw Lake at 10:30 p.m., but with his cell number in hand and a trip to the Town of Northbrook to get a cell connection I reached him about 3:00 p.m. and discovered he was already en route to Bon Echo from Toronto. He was expecting to arrive at 5:00 p.m. With this stroke of good luck I got to the dock, filled my pack with supper, and awaited his arrival.

I had planned on staying overnight in the hut, but the night before I was to meet Geoff I checked the huts book I'd brought along and discovered that it doesn't have sleeping accommodation, just cooking and hanging out. To stay overnight I needed a tent and Thermarest that I didn't have with me as I was camping in my mini van. The hut does have a fireplace and the kitchen is equipped with propane stoves, and the usual things with which an ACC hut comes equipped, plus a sauna near the lake. Chapel Hut on the grounds is a bit of a misnomer as it is really a tool shed. I was in a bit of a quandary as to what to do about sleeping, but Geoff assured me he could ferry me back and forth across the lake when I wished. Therefore, I booked myself into the provincial park campground for two more nights and hustled down to the dock to meet him.

While waiting at the dock I met Karen McGilvray, along with Sam, a girl who works for Karen, with her daughter Twyla, and Lucas, Karen's six year old son, who were getting their gear together to go to the hut. In due course Geoff and a buddy arrived in the ACC boat with his welcoming smile and we all piled in and made the trip across the lake to the hut.

Scattered throughout the woods surrounding the hut are a dozen or so small, recently leveled sites for tents. On my tour around the tents I pined to have my wee tent too <sigh>. Some of the sites have lovely views of Mazinaw Lake.

After arriving at the hut Geoff took off with his climbing buddy on a quick rock climb up a route on the cliffs while I hung out and got to know the others and cooked my dinner. When Geoff returned to the hut he was back and forth across the lake picking up more climbers. It was fun to chat with folks around the fire pit, which adds immeasurably to the ambience, especially to a six-year-old boy who likes roasted marshmallows.

Later in the evening with only the lights across the lake to guide him Geoff took me back to the public dock and I headed to the provincial park campground and my wet campsite with a zillion pine needles sticking to my boots.

Saturday morning I met Geoff at the provincial park dock, a short walk from my campsite, and directly across from the spectacular Mazinaw Rock. He was transporting folks to the cliffs in the Club boat. I was the tourist sitting in the boat, learning about climbing at Bon Echo, and listening to Geoff's enthusiastic running commentary on the different routes. We were back and forth from the hut to the cliffs with various climbers all morning which gave me a great introduction not only as to how folks climb here, but also to absorb the enthusiasm of these die-hard rock climbers, and listen to them talk climbing in a non mountain environment.

This is not at all like the Rockies. I've been a hut custodian in the Rockies, a job with lots of time to climb or hike, but the custodian at Bon Echo Hut has to spend his time ferrying people from the road's public dock to the hut and then from the hut to the cliffs. The unique part about climbing here is that climbers step from the boat onto the rock; there is no approach to the rock. Sitting in the bow of the boat they don their rock shoes, step out, and up they go!

After lunch at the hut I hiked the portage trail through the woods to Kishkebus Lake (1.6 km). This is also canoe country and Canadian Shield country, so there are lots of big rocks. On my return I spent time wandering around looking at all the tents on their little leveled spots, scrambling up a rocky knoll and enjoying the fall colors of the trees and Mazinaw Lake.

Later Geoff came back and took me down the lake to a public dock at the narrows on the cliff side of the lake and I hiked up the tourist trail to the cliff top with the lovely view of the lake.

Spending the evening in the hut cooking dinner, and chatting with the climbers I was thoroughly entertained. Karen, who is very impressive, has her own climbing gym in Toronto. She had brought Sam with her to look after Lucas while she and her climbing partner Katherine were on the rock. There were about 20 people in the hut all keen climbers. I remember Will who is an engineer in the Canadian space program in Ottawa (awesome) as well as people from Toronto, Montreal and.... I only met one fellow who had climbed in the big mountains.

Much later, in the pitch-black night, Geoff took me back across the lake to the provincial park dock (amazing how he finds his way) and with my headlamp on I wandered back to my campsite. This was a bit tricky even though I'd previously plotted my route, as a headlamp is not meant for wandering in the woods. The next day it poured rain and I was glad to be in my dry mini van and not in a tent that I would have to dry out.

All in all it was a wonderful visit to this hut outside of the mountains and I found Geoff to be an enthusiastic, wonderful tour guide to this Rockies gal. My thanks go to him and David Brown for all their help and kindness.

A Guide to Rock Climbs at Bon Echo can be viewed at the ACC library in the Whyte Museum Archives in Banff or the ACC Clubhouse in Canmore or you can check with the Toronto Section as to its whereabouts. It is a beautiful hard cover book with lots of photos and sketches showing the rock climbs plus everything you've ever wanted to know about these spectacular cliffs in Ontario. I recommend a visit the next time you find yourself in Ontario.

What I learned While Lying on my Mat

Published in the Alpine Club of Canada Gazette—Fall 2007

It is well over a year ago that I attended a Mountain Culture Committee meeting as ACC librarian. At the end of the meeting Bob Sandford handed me two old Canadian Alpine Journals along with the scanned copies of them to proof read in preparation for the journals going onto a DVD. By the time I finished proof reading those two journals I was hooked. A year later the last of the scanned journals was done and I had proof read every word of somewhere between forty or fifty journals.

The project helped save my sanity as I lay on my mat on the living room floor awaiting back surgery. I was not bored; I was fascinated. I learned so much about Canada. Not just about climbing in Canada, which in itself is mesmerizing, but about this grand country I live in. The Coast Range, Baffin Island, the St. Elias Mountains, the Rockies, eastern and central Canada, even about mountains in South America, the Himalaya and other places in the world. I also learned a great deal about the people who wrote the articles. It has been a marvellous education I wouldn't have missed for anything.

I also learned how the ACC has changed over the years—by how people wrote in the early years of the Club up to the present, and what those people are like. I read marvellous stories, told in fascinating detail. There are so many good writers in our Club, so many adventurous people doing amazing things. I am fairly knowledgeable about Canada's geography, but I learned so much more along with many specifics, like what the approach to the Cirque of the Unclimbables is like. I climbed those walls, and big mountains and frozen waterfalls along with the writers. I just couldn't stop reading. I even read the latest journals from my collection even though they didn't have to be proofed as they were already in digital form. Of course, over the years I've read a few articles here and there, but not every word. Reading all those words broadened my perspective and education and took me to so many interesting places.

Most of us have heard about the selfish ambitions of climbers on Mount Everest, who pass people in trouble, leaving them to die. Reading our Canadian Alpine Journals introduced me to several heroes and heroines who stopped to help climbers in trouble, and abandoned their summit objectives. Two who stand out are Sylvia Forest and Lisa Paulson who watched three climbers tumble down Mount Huayna Potosi in Bolivia. These two women dropped their hopes of summiting the mountain they had gone so far to achieve, hauled out rescue gear and in a very heroic, professional maneuver immobilized a broken collar bone and got the man with the broken leg lowered down the mountain and saved their lives. It was a different summit they reached that day, the Good Samaritan Summit. They are my heroines. (C.A.J. 2002 pg. 76)

I highly recommend subscribing and reading all of the Canadian Alpine Journals, every word of them. You too can be entertained and educated and meet some interesting people while sitting in your own armchair. And, meet some outstanding heroes—male and female.

Chapter 6

Mountain Trips

Ruthie's Little Hiking Group on the summit of Mount Allan, Kananaskis Country, 2005. Left to right standing: Bruce Heebner, Donna Iddings, Lynda Beyer, Anna Frank, Ken Slemko, Nina Kiiakina, Judith Chubachi and Pierre; kneeling: Drew Holloway and Ruthie. Photo: Jaynett Betts.

Trail Reports

These extensive hiking trip descriptions were initially written for my staff in the Kananaskis Country information centres to help them know about certain backcountry trails.

Sometimes I just have to go on a big hike hence the following trip. However, this trip would never have happened if I had taken the advice I gave to Kananaskis visitors about the high water that existed at the time.

Kananaskis Country Loop

Elbow Lake – Sheep River – Mist Creek Trails, Kananaskis Country
Date: July 20 & 21, 1993
Trailhead: Elbow Pass Day Use on Highway 40
Distance: 6.3 km, 11.9 km, 12 km
Length: 8 hours first day; 6.25 hours second day.

The night before this trip I had camped at Elkwood Campground in Peter Lougheed Provincial Park. I was visiting Millie and George Stefanick who had treated me to dinner the night before and then gave me a pancake breakfast, which definitely gave me an excellent start to a very difficult day.

I started hiking from the Elbow Pass parking lot on Highway 40 at about 10:00 a.m. It was raining but I was fully geared up to withstand it, e.g. rain anorak, rain pants, good Gortex gaiters and leather hiking boots, along with a 30-35 pound pack.

The Elbow Lake Trail has been greatly improved. I remember it being rutted with the creek flowing down the trail. Not any more. It now has a good packed gravel base and neat rocks lining the side of the trail and drainage ditches at various points. I noticed men from the minimum-security prison in a truck at the trailhead, so I assume they are responsible for these wonders. The trail was wet but the packed gravel sections were good. Two hikers caught up with me and chatted a bit, but eventually I lost them as they waited for their friends. I passed two hikers who decided to abort their camping trip and head back to their car. The rain wasn't too heavy, the flowers were out and the peaks were in clouds. It took about a half hour to get to Elbow Lake, a beautiful gem situated at 6,900 feet and surrounded by big peaks and alpine meadows. I could see smoke from some campers in the backcountry campground, but I stayed on the trail around the west side of the lake. Because of this I saw two mule deer in the woods beyond the lake—they were not even skittish. At the same time I noticed a man walking along the other side of the lake who turned out to be a litter picker for the park and we met at the outlet stream from the lake. I was really grateful for this as the logs across the stream were wet, the stream was a couple of feet deep and I didn't want wet feet this early in the hike. The guy passed me his litter-picker-upper to help steady me across the wet logs.

As I followed the trail downstream towards the Sheep Trail I encountered a lot of standing water that was tricky to get around, but as the trail gained elevation it became drier. It also quit raining and the people whom I had met earlier caught up with me—just after I finished having a leak behind a big rock! Good timing. I think these people were chasing me to meet this wonder woman backpacking on her own, because they stayed with me and introduced themselves and asked a lot of questions. They were going to go along the Sheep Trail a bit and when I told them about Rae Lake they decided to go there. I also told them about the old Elbow Lake pack trail which goes off the Sheep Trail and pointed out how to find it. They decided to take it for their route back to Elbow Lake (they were on a day trip). When their two friends caught up with us we continued as a group to the Rae Lake junction where they had a tea stop, giving me some too. I also had my lunch at this spot. The hikers left for the lake and I enjoyed the view that had a lot of cloud cover but some wonderful meadows could be seen across the valley and on Mount Rae.

After lunch I continued along the Sheep Trail gaining elevation to a high point. I took a side trail to the top of a little hill where I got a marvellous view of the two Sheep Lakes that sit on a plateau to the east. I saw a puff of smoke at the north end of the more northerly of the lakes, which I later found was from the Fish and Wildlife cabin.

Continuing along Sheep Trail I got an excellent look into the Rae Creek valley (not the same valley which Rae Lake is in) and it looked wild and wonderful. There doesn't appear to be a trail into it, but there was a rock cairn on the side of the Sheep Trail at the high point, which I suspect Tony and Gillean Daffern erected (*Kananaskis Country Trail Guide*). The Sheep Valley is superb and you really are isolated. I trundled down the trail looking at flowers (sorry Monique, no names) and gazing in wonder at the alpine meadows on the mountains. I couldn't see the peaks for the clouds. A few showers, but nothing horrendous yet. Then I came to the Rae Creek crossing. It wasn't much, so I took off my boots and socks and forded it in bare feet. Put all that lot back on and in another kilometre or so I had to do it all over again. At this second crossing I saw a deserted outfitters' camp in the woods. I didn't investigate the camp as there wasn't any smoke from stoves or fires. It is not easy to get customers in all this rain.

Further down the trail I encountered a major stream crossing—the Sheep River. The water was boiling down the riverbed and running down the trail as well at a terrific rate. I was intimidated to say the least. I felt this necessitated a contemplative sit under a tree and some chocolate cookies. It rained very hard, so I sat for about a half hour trying to decide if I was going to get my feet very wet or camp here. There weren't any spots to camp. I read my map—something I should have done a few days ago—and discovered I had four major river crossings. "Oh well, I might as well do it all today and get it done," I thought. So, I plunged in with a dead tree for a balance stick. Four fords, dragging my dead tree behind me, then add in Burns Creek and map error and it was eight fords altogether. Fortunately, I didn't know this until I finished them all.

After this first major ford, I passed the covered wagons camp and their dog gave me a big scare; I thought he was going to attack me he was growling, snarling and barking so furiously. The girl in the camp called him off in time. Somewhere in this area I saw a very large animal lick just off the trail. There were a lot of game trails leading into it.

On down the trail until I next came to Denny's Cabin on the Burns land. (Owned by the famous Pat Burns since 1903.- I was once here about twenty years ago by car!) Since the cabin, situated at the site of an obviously very deep ford, had smoke coming out of it, I thought I'd get more information about the trail. So I went over and knocked on the cabin door, which woke up three sleepy guys. I inquired about the forthcoming fords and camp spots and they said the ford here was the last one and at the next spot the river ran down the trail, but you could go up the bank and avoid that one. However, the ford at Denny's Cabin was up to the horse's bellies! "But, I'll float away." I said and asked if they would take me across on one of their horses. Instead, one of

Gibraltar, Sheep River
Ford, 1993.

the guys came out of the cabin and scouted the river for me. I trailed behind him, dragging my dead tree—quite the sight. The guy found a place upstream and I asked him to watch me while I forded it. Once more I plunged into that raging river. Plunge is the word! I did make it, but I got bark all over my hands, so I dropped the tree, washed the bark off my hands in the river, and then waved my thanks to the guys. The other two had come out of the cabin to watch. Just like a scene from the movies. The river roaring along between us drowned out any chance of yelling thanks, so my wave had to do.

In a short time I could see another camp further off the trail, but I didn't go into it, just continued on my way. Then I came to the spot the guys had mentioned where the river ran down the trail. This time it was even bigger and really roaring along in a threatening way, however, I did find the trail along the mountainside that avoided the river. Then I came to the ford. A spot where there used to be a bridge over the river, but now there were two logs wired together and one was partially broken in the middle, so it had a dip in it. The river was deep and I knew this was not for me. Not even the logs. They were wet, probably slippery, and a terror to inch across on your butt with a backpack on. So, I decided to camp for the night and make a decision in the morning.

As luck would have it, when scouting for a campsite, I came across another river crossing further upstream, one that the horses obviously used and which was not as deep. Very scary though as the river was just tearing along at a great pace, bubbling and muddy so I couldn't see the bottom, and rolling the rocks on the bottom. It was definitely not as deep as the former bridge site, but it was 6:00 p.m. and I was tired after eight hours on the trail. This was not a good time to do a major ford. Since I thought the river might go down overnight (a common occurrence) I found the only possible place to put a small tent—on some gravel about fifteen feet from the river. It had quit raining, so I got my tent up and gear stowed away and made some dinner. This turned out to be a rather nice spot to camp. The view from my tent of Burns Mountain was just lovely. The clouds had lifted and some blue sky was showing to the south. I sat cross-legged inside the front of the tent, on my soft Thermarest mattress and enjoyed the view. I prayed it wouldn't rain in the night so that the river would go down. I knew that early in the morning the river would be at its lowest if it didn't rain, so I planned to get up at 6:00 a.m. and cross before breakfast.

Going to sleep was not an easy job. I was so scared of that river. I had to get up about 2:00 a.m., so checked the river to see if it had gone down. During the previous evening I'd noted two rocks, one on each side of the river, and I was watching them for water levels; using the rocks as guides. When I checked the rocks at 2:00 a.m., I could see the river had gone down a little. I slept better after that. I woke up again at 6:15 a.m. The first thing I realized was that it had not rained in the night and although I could hear the roar of the river it sounded less ominous. Since I was still scared I put off getting up for a half hour. Finally, I decided I'd better do it, so I got out of my sleeping bag and rummaged around in the tent packing up my gear. I was scared to look at the river until I was ready to cross it, so although my tent was fifteen feet from the river, I studiously avoided glancing in that direction. No sense in scaring myself any more than I was! I had my shorts on as I didn't want to get my long pants wet. At 7:20 a.m. I grabbed my courage and the dead tree I'd salvaged the night before, broke all the branches off the tree, and walked over to the river. It had lost its muddy look and I could see the deepest spot was nearer the other side and then it was much shallower. This boded well because if I stumbled I could reach the bottom of the shallow bit with my hands and not get my whole body wet. So, I said another prayer and went for it. When I was in the deepest spot I could tell I was going to make it even though the water was up to the bottoms of my shorts.

I made it! What a relief.

I walked a couple of hundred yards to the junction with Mist Creek Trail, so I was sure of where I was, and then walked back to the river, so I could have water for my breakfast tea. I changed into dry clothes, and found some big trees to cook under and ended up quite comfortable.

Since I had lots of time I didn't rush breakfast. I had to meet Katie Scott on top of Rickert's Pass between one and two in the afternoon. I started up Mist Creek Trail just after 8:00 a.m. En route I saw evidence of the Burns coal mining days. It took two grueling hours to reach the top of Rickert's Pass. Very steep—about 1900 feet elevation gain. With a heavy pack it was some grunt. The alpine meadows around the bowl you enter to reach the pass are really superb. I could see an animal lick with game trails going to it. Unfortunately, I took my last photo just before the pass.

Rickert's Pass is very narrow, only about 50 feet wide, with rocky ridges on both sides. It is very spectacular, with a superb view in two directions, and you can scramble up the ridges on either side and get an even better view. The pass is about 7600 feet high. Of course, with my early morning start, I arrived there just after 10:00 a.m. With Katie (who was working for me at Kananaskis Village Information Centre) not arriving until sometime between 1:00 p.m. and 2:00 p.m., I had lots of time to spare. The weather was clearing and the sun was coming out, so I found shelter from the wind and sat eating my chocolate cookies and finished off my bag of cherries. A herd of ten sheep crossed the pass just below me and scrambled over the ridges to far meadows. Two little lambs scampered after their mothers like it was nothing at all.

As long as the weather was nice I didn't mind waiting for Katie. We had made an agreement on time, but also an alternate plan of action if the weather was bad, to leave two cairns so one would know the other had gone down. I scrambled up the ridge to the north now and then to look across to the south to see if I could see her coming.

The long wait ended up being a blessing, as I was able to observe the small creatures doing their thing: three pikas, several chipmunks and Columbian ground squirrels all scampering around in search of food. They were quite oblivious of me as I was very quiet. (No screaming and yelling to scare off bears for me.) I highly recommend sitting on a pass for three hours. You can really take in the scenery and the wildlife to a degree not possible when continuously hiking or when you only spend twenty minutes on a pass. I enjoyed the big mountains to the east and west and the wonderful meadows on Mist Ridge and at the base of Mist Mountain.

I could also see where a lightning fire had occurred on a ridge to the east of Mist Mountain. It all remains fresh in my mind. It was a high point in more ways than one.

By the time I'd eaten lunch and spent two and a half hours on the pass I was impatient to be moving, so I scrambled up the ridge for one last look for Katie. Suddenly there she was in the distance, coming across the highest points of Mist Ridge—obviously making good time. I was so excited I took off up the ridge to meet her and there in a sea of alpine flowers, with the wind gaily blowing, we met. After my tremendous river crossings, and for Katie her route finding across the high Mist Ridge, we were both really happy to see each other. (There is always the nagging thought the other might have canned out.) Back at the pass Katie had some lunch, shared her tea, and regaled me with her adventures and I told her mine. Then we hiked down the Mist Creek Trail nattering away the whole time.

Mist Creek Trail leaves the alpine meadows rather quickly and enters the trees. It was good walking for a distance, but then we started encountering lots of mud and some minor stream crossings; then more and more mud and then marsh. By this time I was saying "Oh what the heck" and just tromping through the marsh. We eventually met some girls from Camp Chief Hector (YMCA). One cute little girl said, "Welcome to our world." They seemed to be having fun, in spite of the mud. We also came across their tent camp in a dry area further down the trail.

The first part of this trail is in a fir forest and the lower section in a lodge pole pine forest, probably reminiscent of the Phillip's fire in 1936. The trail is well marked at the junction of the Mist Ridge route (an unmarked trail up an old exploration road before getting onto the ridge) and it is also well marked at the crossing of the old forestry trunk road. It then crosses Highway 40 and goes along close to Mist Creek to the Mist Creek day use site. We were lucky; the sun followed us all the way down from Rickert's Pass to the parking lot. After cloud and rain this was pretty nice. I splayed out on the pavement for a short rest before Katie drove me back to my truck and we met again at Fortress Junction for a snack.

As mentioned previously, I had driven the Sheep River Trail (once an old fire road) about 1973 and I must say anything I hiked that long ago I remember pretty well, but I don't remember anything but Denny's Cabin from that car trip.

I highly recommend this hike during high water to crazies and people wishing a real challenge at river crossings, bearing in mind you could drown. At low water times of year it would be an ideal long two-day hike. I did learn what life is like along the Sheep River during high water and it will prove useful in the future. It is also fascinating to see rivers in full flood; it is so easy to be deceived when you hike only in dry weather. I also found I got a real adrenaline rush each time I successfully forded that raging river—an interesting and unexpected phenomena. It's so nice to be alive!

Another Kananaskis Loop

Burstall Pass - Palliser Pass - North Kananaskis Pass
Trailhead: Burstall Pass parking lot on the Smith-Dorrien/Spray Trail road
Trails: Burstall Pass-Upper Spray River-Palliser River-Leroy Creek, Maude-Lawson Trail to North Interlakes parking lot.
Length of Trail: 15.2 km, 10.2 km, 13.8 km, 15.0 km
Elevation Gain/Loss: lots
Date: August 13-16, 1993

On August 13th Trish Jevne (55), her brother Denis Reist (57), and Ruthie (56) left Burstall Pass parking lot in Kananaskis Country at 11:30 a.m. after signing out at Barrier Lake Visitor Information Centre, and leaving Trish's car at North Interlakes parking lot. It was a warm, sunny day and the going was easy until we crossed the Dryas Flats with its view of the Robertson Glacier. Asters, arnica and valerian bloomed along the trail and the mountains looked lovely in the sunlight after many days of rain. We passed nineteen people, including Bob Reynolds the former regional director of Kananaskis Country in Canmore, who was with one of my Barrier Lake Visitor Centre visitors, whose face I recognized. We said hello to everyone we met and had a short chat with Bob and his two friends. We had lunch in the shelter of some trees on the last level area before the final ascent to the pass. I had forgotten how really nice Burstall Pass is on a sunny day. Superb. Flowers blooming, mountains shining in the sun and spectacular hills and dales amongst it all. The summit of this very wide pass is the boundary with Banff National Park.

We didn't make any side trips for views, so had no problem finding the trail over the pass, however the view of Leman Lake in Banff Park is outstanding and the views of the Upper Spray Valley as we descended the pass were awesome. There were lots of meadows throughout the whole Spray Valley, although we discovered later they were really willow bushes and other scrub bushes, but it looked great from up high. There are very good, large cairns on the Banff Park side of the trail as you descend the pass. The cairns are through a rocky meadow with fabulous views of the peaks and an interesting sinkhole. The trail becomes more evident as it goes into the trees, traverses in a southerly direction and then down the ridge. Where the trail dropped down the wild rhododendron bushes that surround it were in full bloom. Close to the Upper Spray River the trail switches to a northerly direction and goes, what seems a long way, in that direction before meeting the Upper Spray River Trail. It is a big drop down to this trail. From the junction of the two trails we travelled downstream to the backcountry campsite. This last bit seems to take forever. En route, and not long before you reach the campsite, you pass the warden's cabin flying its Canadian flag. (No one was in it when we passed by.)

I had picked up the required camping permit from the Banff Park Information Centre a couple of days before the hike. The campsite is not used often, so I was told in the information centre, and sure enough you could tell from the plant growth on the tent pad sites. We found a couple of spots for our tents and we quickly erected them as it was 6:00 p.m. when we arrived and we were tired. We made dinner (Trish and I had each brought two dinners for the trip.) There are fire pits at this campsite, so Trish and Denis got a fire going while I cooked and pretty soon we were feeling mellow. As the day became dusk and we were sitting around the fire a deer came and browsed very close. Later when I got into my sleeping bag I could hear him chewing beside my tent.

The next morning we rose around 7:00 a.m. and Denis, who was up first, spotted five moose not far down the valley to the north. They were probably the reason the deer chose us for company. There was a lovely view of the Spray River Valley from our campsite even though it is in trees for shelter. We were on the trail by 9:50 a.m. and retraced our steps back to the Burstall Pass Trail junction, but continued on the Upper Spray River Trail towards Palliser Pass. Just 0.02 km beyond the Burstall Pass Trail turnoff was the turnoff for Leman Lake (not as indicated on the topographic map). It is only one km to Leman Lake, but we took a vote and decided to bypass it as we had seen it from the top of Burstall Pass. There is a bridge over the Spray River to reach Leman Lake – it was the last bridge we saw for the next 2.5 days.

We continued on the Upper Spray River Trail and at one point stopped for a rest. While stopped I heard a rustle in the bush ahead and later we discovered fresh bear scat. The bear must have heard us and cleared out of the way. At the base of Palliser Pass we stopped for lunch where we could enjoy the view back down the valley. It is very spectacular mountain scenery with wildflowers blooming at our feet—valerian, fleabane, arnica, cinquefoil, etc. As it was breezy we put on our jackets and we started up the pass through the trees and rhododendron bushes.

Palliser Pass, while intimidating from the higher reaches of Burstall Pass Trail, is not that high. About 500 feet of elevation gain. It was rather warm hiking so when the bushes offered a small open spot I declared in a loud voice "I'm going to take my jacket off right here."

Great Rolls of Thundeeeerrrr!!!!!

"Okay I won't take my jacket off."

Within five minutes it started to rain and I was glad I hadn't taken my pack off, taken the jacket off, put the pack back on, and then had to repeat the process all over.

As the trail leveled out we came to Belgium Lake with Mount Queen Elizabeth above it with a nice sized glacier and a beautiful waterfall cascading down to the lake. Belgium Lake had meadows around two sides and there was another little, unnamed lake on the left hand side of the trail—Belgium Lake being on the right hand side of the trail. It should be noted that the trail on the topographic map is not in the proper position.

Belgium Lake is on the Alberta side of Palliser Pass. Back Lake and Palliser Lake are on the British Columbia side of the pass. When we reached Palliser Pass there was a man-made boundary cairn with "British Columbia" on one side and "Alberta" on the other. There was also a Banff National Park sign and a Height of the Rockies Wilderness Area sign on the British Columbia side. The beautiful meadows shone in the sun, with wonderful views of Mounts Sir Douglas, Williams, Munro, LeRoy, Back, Queen Elizabeth and King Albert on the Continental Divide as it zigzagged over the height of land.

Without any difficulty Denis found a small trail leading to Back Lake, so we hiked along that with the intent to camp there. When we arrived we discovered massive grizzly bear diggings and a gorgeous aqua coloured lake with a beautiful waterfall dropping into it. Since we hadn't flushed any bears out of the small cirque by our presence we felt it was safe to camp. It was obvious the bear had been and was gone. (Maybe he was the one we heard in the Upper Spray Valley.) Where the bear hadn't messed up the terrain there was a nice meadow, although it was lumpy and difficult to find a camping spot, but very pretty.

We did manage to find a spot for the two tents, albeit my feet were between two big plant-covered rocks. Fortunately, I have a miniscule tent. We decided to have our campfire on the largest bear digging where we couldn't do any more damage.

After dinner (Trish cooked her marvellous spaghetti) we were standing around the fire when I looked up on the hillside and suddenly realized the white spots I could see were goats—ten of them! We watched as they climbed up to the base of the cliff on Mount Queen Elizabeth and then bedded down for the night. The cliff at their backs and the slope dropping away below them on three sides showed good safety strategy. After we crawled in our tents for the night I sat cross-legged in the doorway of mine and watched the mountains gathering in the dusk. It was a very peaceful spot. That night I had the best sleep I'd had in a long time.

The next morning the clouds hung over the tops of the mountains, but the weather didn't actually look that bad. We packed up and headed down the Back Lake Trail to Palliser Pass (about one km), and then followed the Palliser River Trail into British Columbia and the Palliser River. We passed a small pond and then Palliser Lake—another beauty with a narrow drop at the end of the lake and a bit of meadow along one edge. From Palliser Lake the trail climbed uphill for a short distance before starting its descent into the Palliser River valley. On the way down, the trail forked and, thinking it met again in a minute, I led us onto the right hand fork. This turned out to be the older of the two trails and was very over hung with rhododendron bushes. It did hook up with the other trail, but much further down. The spot where the two trails met was the last possible camping spot on the British Columbia side of our trip. From there onwards it was bushwhacking on a trail, getting wetter and wetter and fording the creek sized Palliser River twice. Good bear country, so I did a lot of yodeling. When Denis first heard me yodel he thought "What the h…. is going on?" When he realized what I was yodeling about he said, "Keep it up, keep it up."

The trail followed the river through rhododendron bushes, willow bushes, big trees, cow parsnip, black current bushes, and even a few blueberries (usually blueberries are only found in British Columbia in this part of the Rockies). Earlier we had found a few strawberries on the steeper section of Palliser Pass. We could pick the black currents and blueberries as we walked down the trail.

From the top of the last high point on Palliser Pass I had viewed the landscape of the Palliser valley, noting Mount LeRoy and which ridge we would have to go around to find LeRoy Creek. As we hiked down the valley I watched that ridge from the open spots, as I didn't want to miss the turnoff. (I remembered that a visitor to Barrier Lake Visitor Centre had told me they missed the LeRoy Creek Trail turn off and had to do some backtracking.)

As the day wore on it started to rain lightly, which continued all day. This made us evaluate whether or not to follow our original intention of doing a side trip to Tipperary Lake. We decided against doing that as it would be a 1000 foot climb and we were not sure about (a) a trail and (b) which side of Tipperary Creek it was on. This meant we had to hike all the way to Turbine Canyon in one day. If there had been a spot to camp on LeRoy Creek we would have done so, but the bush did not allow for this, so we trudged on. We eventually came to the end of Mount LeRoy ridge. Since we didn't want to miss the turnoff to LeRoy Creek, we stopped for lunch in a very small clearing. Then we did the tough bushwhack down to the Palliser River, forded the river (easy but wet) and bushwhacked up the other side and continued bushwhacking until we came across the LeRoy Creek Trail. Oh joy! We followed this trail up the creek valley until we came to where the trail must have crossed the creek; however, on the other side we could not find the trail. We followed the rocky creek and finally found what turned out to be a game trail up the mountainside away from LeRoy Creek, but towards the North Kananaskis Pass. We couldn't see the actual pass as we headed up this slope, but I was pretty sure we were in the right place as I had reviewed my topographic map the night before, so when I was feeling a bit unsure of myself I just kept thinking we had to be right.

Seventeen years before I had come down the North Kananaskis Pass and over the shoulder of a mountain towards Beatty Creek and gone up Beatty Creek to the South Kananaskis Pass. I had identified the shoulder of that mountain, although it looked much higher than I remembered. (There was a marvellous, huge spring of water coming out of the foliage on this shoulder—cascading in a great waterfall down the mountainside.) Finally, after the game trail petered out and we were bushwhacking once more, we got to a high point where we could see the North Kananaskis Pass. Gosh, it was high and forbidding—higher than I remembered. Once more I wondered if I was right. I kept my thoughts to myself as my two companions were not very good route finders.

We continued climbing uphill and traversing (I was hoping if it was the wrong pass that at least we could camp on the other side.) Soon, I was reassured we were in the right place as I could see a waterfall that I remembered from seventeen years ago coming out of the rock below the pass. It drains from Maude Lake, which is lower than the North Kananaskis Pass. Actually Maude Lake drains to the Pacific Ocean and the Atlantic Ocean. As we were traversing and climbing towards the pass I noticed something that looked like a trail, so we headed towards it and sure enough, in spite of some awful bushwhacking, it was the trail. Oh joy! Denis heaved an enormous sigh of relief, as he had been very skeptical this was the right place. He was thoroughly impressed with my tenaciousness and persistence in finding this trail.

Our work was still not over as the trail was very, very steep and we were very, very tired. It went up and up and up, it seemed forever. We struggled on, getting more and more tired, the time getting later and later. We crossed the dry creek bed above the waterfall and went through some big trees—then a rest stop, then a breather, until finally we broke out of the scrub bush and onto the meadows of the pass.

What a welcome sight Maude Lake was even though it was shrouded in cloud and barely visible. The sign saying provincial park boundary showed we had entered Peter Lougheed Provincial Park, part of Kananaskis Country. The pass is 7682 feet. We followed the trail down the pass, around the scree slope above Maude Lake and over the hills and dales of the pass area. Beatty Glacier looming above us on Mount Beatty, beautiful and awesome, it looked on us benevolently. Down and down the pass we went—just two kilometres from the pass to Turbine Canyon backcountry campsite—would it ever come? The clouds hung lower until we couldn't see the mountains, but the hills and dales coming off the pass were really lovely. Lush and green, wet and still—then the campsite. "Oh, you welcome thing." Off with the packs at last—ten hours since we started out! Are we tough or what? Up with the tents—some of the tent pad sites had pools of water on them, but we managed to find two that had drainage ditches dug around them; into the shelter of the trees to cook dinner in the misty cloud. Not rain now, just the mist of the cloud we were in. And then falling into the sleeping bags in welcome relief.

"Morning Denis, what's the weather doing out there?"

"Same as last night."

"Oh drats."

The night before we had decided if the weather was good in the morning we would stay over a day at Turbine Canyon and mosey around, but if the weather was bad, we would hike out to the car at North Interlakes parking lot. We were really too tired to hike out, so after breakfast in the shelter of the trees, we walked over to the canyon and had a look at it. I had been here four or five times, but Denis and Trish had never seen it.

Turbine Canyon is one of the most spectacular canyons you will find in the Rockies. It must be eighty to one hundred feet deep in places, and very narrow. There is a spot at the top where you can jump across, and a marvellous waterfall drops into this crack and cascades down the canyon at a great rate.

Occasionally the clouds moved around and we could see some of the peaks, but they really did settle in to stay for awhile, so we packed up our gear and headed down the trail, past Lawson Lake with its black rock and lack of fish, through lush green alpine vegetation, mixed with larch trees, some of which had already started turning orange, up a rise on the other side of Lawson Lake and around the slope overlooking an unnamed pond with a lone duck in it, down a steep grade and across the flat area emanating out of a cirque on Mount Putnik and Mount Beatty. Down some more. We were just putting on our packs after a rest when Trish said, "Look".

"What, another nut!" I exclaimed. Yes, a young guy hoofing it up the trail with a grin on his face. It turned out he works at the OCO Haig Glacier ski camp and he was going back after his days off to work his next five days. He was the first person we had seen in three days—since Burstall Pass.

The trail continued to drop down—muddy is the word—with switchbacks through three avalanche slopes. I couldn't see much, but was too tired to yodel. Raining. Hood up, head down, "OK yes, and look up once in awhile" and on we go. Finally we reached the Forks backcountry campground where we planned to have lunch. Rain or not, we got out the stove and brewed up some soup, tea and hot chocolate and took a much needed rest.

This campsite is in big trees with a view of the Upper Kananaskis River from some of the sites. Fire pits and firewood. I don't recommend an axe in the backcountry. It's too easy to chop a body part accidentally.

On we trudge, with those heavy packs on our backs (mine was 36 lbs. when I started out and 31 lbs. when I returned), over the Upper Kananaskis River on a nice bridge at a canyon and waterfall (I told Denis and Trish about when we used to have to ford the river or cross on a log jamb). We walked in forest, quite thick with lots of bearberry flowers and arnica. We were sitting down having a rest, amidst the mud puddles on the trail, when two groups of two guys come jogging down the trail in the direction we had come. Lycra pants!

Trish: "Where are your skis?" She sure caught on quickly to where they came from—more OCO skiers from Haig Glacier. We cross the bridge over the last creek, climbed the hill onto the old fire road (built in the early 1970s to put out a forest fire) and on over the rocks of Mount Indefatigable. There are great views of the Upper Kananaskis Lake and in the direction where Aster Lake lies hidden. The clouds are a little higher now, or are we a little lower? Raspberries! Marvellous. Too tired to bend down, too tired to take the pack off and eat berries. On we hike. We're almost there. Mount Indefatigable Trail turnoff and we are finally at the Interlakes Dam. Cross the dam and we are at the parking lot. Almost 6:00 p.m. and we started out at 11:00 a.m. Tired—that's an understatement.

We drove back to Burstall Pass parking lot to get my truck. Trish and Denis drove north up the Smith-Dorrien/Spray Trail road to Canmore and Trish's daughter's shower and I drove north up Highway 40 to drop off our backcountry slip at Barrier Lake Visitor Information Centre.

Wow the rain is heavier and heavier the further north I drive. The creeks are in full spring-like flood and brown. We got off lightly with the rain. It was never this heavy while we were hiking.

I showered and changed at home in Exshaw, then met Trish and Denis at Bing's Restaurant in Canmore at 9:00 p.m. for Chinese dinner. I've never seen three plates of food and one big bowl of rice demolished in such a flash. There wasn't a speck left!

In retrospect: I've been trying to get to Tipperary Lake for seventeen years. It may always be the lake of my dreams, elusive forever. After the hard last two days of our hike I've decided to grow up and start acting my age before I die in the B.C. bush somewhere! Knowing me, this could be "famous last words."

Trywhitt Loop

Kananaskis Country - July 12, 1994.

It was a crisp morning as we left our vehicles at the parking lot on top of Highwood Pass, on Highway 40. At 7,239 feet (2206.3 meters) Highwood Pass is the highest pass you can drive over in Canada.

We started off on the Highwood Meadows Trail, but left it in just a couple of minutes for the unmarked trail into the woods and the Little Highwood Valley. Our goal was to hike the Tyrwhitt Loop and maybe get up Mount Tyrwhitt. We knew it was 12 km long, but how long it would take us was going to be a surprise.

We were five in number: Ed Silver, a University of Calgary professor, his colleague Tom Grossman, recently from California, Rob Wolfe, my co-worker at the Barrier Lake Information Centre, Graham Walker, a friend of mine from the Alpine Club and Edmonton, and me.

It didn't take us long to get through the woods and into alpine meadows by a small pond. The day was starting to warm up, so we all took off some of our clothes and had a drink from our water bottles. The mountains were surrounding us as we were well into the Little Highwood basin and the views were really wonderful.

Continuing along the trail, which was becoming faint, we could easily see where to go through the open meadows and rocks. Scrambling over some of the rocks was easy. Soon we could see Grizzly Col and the trail on the left hand side ascending to it; it looked tougher than it actually ended up being. We picked our way over snow and rock and scrambled up to the trail above us. This trail took us directly to the col where we had superb views down both sides. To the south we could see a small lake surrounded by beautiful meadows and to the north we could see more meadows and Little Highwood Pass. (I once did a hike to that pass with Jamie Carpenter, another co-worker, and once a ski trip by myself.) It had only taken us two hours to reach Grizzly Col, so we had a rest and some of our munchies. Tom, one of the younger members of the party, ate a lot of munchies; in fact, he spent most of the hike eating munchies! While Graham lolled around on the col, Ed took off up the ridge to the east and Rob, Tom and I headed up Mount Tyrwhitt to see if we could reach the Tyrwhitt Arch and the top of the peak.

The scramble up Mount Tyrwhitt started out well, but soon deteriorated into loose rock on rock and hard packed earth with rocks strewn on top. In some places we actually had to climb with hands and feet. Tom and Rob went to the left, but I continued in a more or less straight line upwards. I was too busy watching my footing to keep a close eye on the guys and for awhile they were lost to my sight, however, they did reach the arch before me, which gave me the incentive to continue in spite of the terrible loose terrain and the actual rock climbing I had to do.

The Arch was eventually reached and I was impressed! A fantastic view through this splendid hole in the rock to the valley below and the highway, and further away the ridge that emanates off Mount Elpoca. The whole thing was awe-inspiring. The arch was like a frame for the view. Trees, meadows and spectacular peaks going off in the distance had us enthralled.

At this point Tom and Rob decided to continue to the summit of the peak, but I'd had enough of this awful rock, so I headed back down using my pole to help me. It had been a big help on the way up, except for the sections I had to put my hand through the wrist loop to use both hands to hang onto the rock. I did manage to get down without a lot of difficulty by being very, very careful and taking my time. I could see Graham and Ed below, waiting on the col.

When I reached them it was a relief to be back on firmer footing, and to sit down for a drink and more munchies. Eventually Rob and Tom arrived back and told me that from the arch to the summit was a lot easier than the section to the arch; however, I didn't really regret not going further. We still had a long way to go on this hike and I'd probably need the energy.

From the col we had to traverse a ridge in a southerly direction. The ridge was beautiful. The alpine flowers were amazing and in great profusion. Except for the side hill gouging, traversing the ridge was relatively easy, but it brought on wild stories from everyone about side hill gougers, their habits and leg lengths. The stories got rather carried away, revealing that in spite of higher education some people can become very silly! While crossing a rockslide I found the rock to be very unstable and, even though I tried to be careful, at one point I stepped with my left foot on a rock and moved my right foot forward as one would normally do, using my pole for balance, when the left rock moved forward and thrust me into a higher rock in front of my foot. I bashed my leg above the ankle on this rock and only caught myself with my pole. By gar, that hurt! I quickly sat down, yelled and moaned and groaned while the four guys stood looking at me in concern, and Ed kept saying: "But she recovers very quickly" giving an account of my rapid recovery when I caught a foot in a ground squirrel hole below Piper Pass some years before. I managed to finish my moaning and groaning (i.e. the pain let up) and was able to continue hiking for another eight hours.

Hiking along the ridge gave us a really marvellous view in all directions, especially when we got right up on the top of the ridge. At one point Rob and I ended up together and lost sight of the others. We did catch up with Ed so continued on together hoping we would see them. Going down the end of the ridge we spied the small group of people who had left the parking lot at the same time we had (they were doing the loop in reverse). Eventually we picked up a small trail traversing down the opposite side of the ridge in the direction we wanted to go, so we followed it and soon saw the other members of our party. We regrouped at the bottom before starting up the next ridge. By now we were getting tired, but we had to climb 300 metres or so to the top of this ridge. This required some bushwhacking, which wasn't fun. The day wasn't too warm so I had left my long pants on which protected me from the rough bush. At the top of the ridge we had another rest and another snack of munchies and waited for Graham. From here we traversed along the top of the ridge in a northerly direction until we were right above the parking lot we had started out from in the morning. We still had to get down the ridge at least 300 metres. We carefully picked our way through the boulders and scree and arrived at the parking lot eleven hours after leaving it. Right on our heels was the group who had gone in the opposite direction, but they had not climbed Mount Tyrwhitt.

I took off my boots and socks to change into my runners and discovered I had a big lump on my leg from my fall. I had been favoring it all day, but didn't realize it was so big. In spite of my injury, it was a marvellous day. Nothing but good old sun and vast mountain ranges in all directions. Being on top of a mountain is one of the most exhilarating moments in life: the view is always fantastic and the thrill is, well thrilling. It makes me realize how very small I am. Helps to get life in perspective.

Tombstone Lakes

Kananaskis Country – July 13-14, 1994.

The day after hiking Tyrwhitt Loop I took off for a couple of days backpack hiking with Trish Jevne and Angela Ovens. Our goal was the Tombstone backcountry campground and Tombstone Lakes. While I have been in the area close to Tombstone Lakes several times in recent years, it was actually about sixteen or seventeen years since I had seen Tombstone Lakes themselves. The trail starts a few kilometres north of Highwood Pass (Elbow Pass parking) and takes a half hour to get to Elbow Lake. Beyond the lake it is largely open meadows, trees and fantastic mountain views. The wildflowers here are outstanding.

When we arrived at the Tombstone campground Trish—as usual—got a fire going and I found the stream for the tea water. Our campsite had a marvellous view of the Misty Range, so we felt we were camping in luxury.

After supper Trish and Angela hiked up to the lakes to fish while I lazed around and nursed my sore leg. Angela found a fishing rod and Trish caught two rainbow trout. We cooked the trout over the fire in the dwindling daylight and enjoyed the quiet evening.

Afterwards Angela and I squeezed into my wee tent and Trish into hers and we listened to the stream trickling in the distance.

The next morning all three of us went to the lakes so I could see them once again and Trish could try her hand at more fishing. It was interesting to see the lakes after so many years. The ridge above the upper lake which Rod Magee and I had climbed was still there, but after my eleven hour hike a couple of days before, I wasn't up to scrambling up it again. The spot where Peggy, Rod and I had pitched our two tents was not at all a likely looking tent site, but I don't recall being uncomfortable. (Peggy and Rod are mother and son; Rod was 15 years old at the time.)

Once more Trish caught two fish (the daily limit) and when we got back to our campsite we cooked them over the fire for lunch. Delicious.

After the fish we packed up our gear and were soon back on the Elbow Lake Trail. Along the way we met up with two guys who were working on the bear study and had trapped and tagged a young black bear near Rae Creek. There were a few fishermen at Elbow Lake. It had been an easy hike and was Angela's first backpack hike. She did just fine and was hooked!

Carnarvon Lake

Kananaskis Country - August 17 and 18, 1994.

High in the mountains of Kananaskis Country, on the boundary of Alberta and British Columbia, lies Carnarvon Lake. Access to the lake is for those who are not intimidated by heights, as a cliff has to be climbed to reach the lake from Alberta, or a very long approach from the British Columbia side.

I drove south on Highway 40 over Highwood Pass to the Cat Creek day use area. Looking north I could see a huge, boiling rain storm blowing my way, so I cancelled all thoughts of going to the lake and drove down the highway to Highwood Junction and had a piece of Laurie Powell's famous chocolate cake. Then I toured through Cataract Creek Campground, but wasn't inclined to stay there. While trying to decide what I wanted to do I looked north and could see the wild storm had passed and the sky was clear and blue. I drove back to Cat Creek.

Before I had time to change my mind I grabbed my pack, hoisted it on my back and headed up the trail to the Highwood River. Cattle grazing is permitted in this area as part of Kananaskis Country's multi-use philosophy. In the three kilometres to the Highwood River I passed several cattle peacefully munching. I had come prepared to ford the river at the crossing by wearing an old pair of runners and socks and carrying my hiking boots. The river was swift, but not too deep. I continued on the trail the short distance to the next ford at McPhail Creek. Once over this creek I took off the runners and socks, put on my hiking socks and boots and hung the wet stuff in a tree to dry until I returned the next day.

From here it was just a straight hike up an old logging road, watching for the turnoff for the lake. Since I had not been here before I occasionally got off on the wrong track and was glad I found my way again. After three hours hiking I really got off on the wrong track. I discovered Gwen Wolfe's concept of a small trail and my concept of a small trail are very different! I should have clarified that with her. Because of this I spent an hour on the wrong old logging road. It had a narrow trail on it, but much too narrow for the actual trail and I got far too high. From where this logging road ended I could see the headwall I had to climb to get to Carnarvon Lake and it was obvious I was in the wrong place. I had to retrace my steps because the bushwhacking looked dreadful and would probably lengthen, rather than shorten the hike. Eventually I did find the right trail.

Soon I started encountering lots of very fresh, wet bear scat. Scat full of juicy red berries! A sane person would have turned back at this point, but I'd come a long way and I've tried for years to see Carnarvon Lake, so I wasn't inclined to go back home. I solved my dilemma by doing a lot of yodeling as I hiked—just to let Mr. Bear know I was around. Fortunately, he must have been busy with the berries as I never did see him.

I finally got to the edge of the trees where I could see the trail climbing up through the scree to the base of the headwall I had to climb. It was a strenuous trek up the scree as I was very tired by this time; it was 5:00 p.m. and my pack seemed to be getting heavier. Going up the headwall was tricky, it was a long way down and there was loose rock on top of the solid rock. I had to be very careful. Half way up I encountered the chain on the cliff, which is to

Andy looking over Carnarvon Lake, 1994.

help you get up, and I stashed my walking stick, an old ski pole, under the cliff. It was getting in my way and becoming treacherous. Standing at this midway spot on the cliff and looking down to where I'd go if I fell, I just about aborted the climb up to the lake. It looked just as scary to go back down! Grabbing my courage I continued up the cliff using the chain to help me. It was a great relief to get to the top!

Looking across the lake I could see a tent on the other side so I knew I wasn't going to be alone. Then, just when I thought I was over the tough stuff and onto easy ground, I found I had to clamber over more rock and down-climb a bit of cliff with the lake below to fall into should I slip, but I made it and followed the trail around the lake to the camping spot.

When I arrived I met two guys and discovered they had been hiking ahead of me on the trail and had only been at the lake about a half hour. They had also seen the bear scat. We chatted and they seemed very nice and definitely friendly. It was about six o'clock, so I quickly got my tent up. One of the guys went fishing and the other helped me move some rocks to act as a windshield for my stove and I started dinner—the usual noodles in sauce from Mr. Lipton.

After dinner I lazed around and rested as I was very tired. It's amazing how tired you can be and still be drawn to roam around and look at the territory. About eight o'clock I started meandering and found a little path up a grass and rock gully to the plateau above the lake. The plateau had meadows and flowers on it and I couldn't resist walking higher and higher to get a better view of the lake and the mountains to the east through the gap made by the two mountains on either side of the lake. This is a very dramatic lake. Huge mountains rising on both sides, the headwall I'd come up at the east end of the lake with a big drop to the valley below, and the plateau and more mountains on the west. Actually, standing on this plateau, which you could call a flat ridge, you are standing on the Continental Divide—the boundary of British Columbia and Alberta.

As I wandered along the ridge I noticed a goat up high and just settling down for the night. Then my eye caught another goat, much closer and moving along a ridge of the mountain above me. I quickly grabbed my camera out of my pocket. He was so close he could hear the click of the camera and stopped in his tracks and looked at me. He wouldn't move until I started moving away from him. Then he walked along the ridge, going a little higher and found a place where he settled down for the night. He had a goat's eye view of the whole area.

Since it was getting dark, I scrambled back down the ridge to my tent and crawled inside my sleeping bag. Lying on my stomach I enjoyed the last of the fading light and the view across the lake to the mountains.

The next morning I could hear Jim and Andy, but I just rolled over and kept on sleeping. When the sun hit the tent it definitely was time to get up. I enjoyed a quiet breakfast before the guys came back from fishing. We decided we would go up the ridge that I was on the night before and look for fossils as Jim said there were some on the mountain on the south side of the lake. So we scrambled up the mountainside for a bit, and pretty soon Andy and I were going higher and higher. Wow! What a great view of the lake! Jim did catch up when we got to an interesting bit of rock sitting by itself. Andy and I continued higher until I decided to call it quits as it was tricky scree on rock with bits of cliff here and there, and I knew I needed some energy for the hike back to my truck.

Reluctantly we scrambled back down to the ridge and then noticed an unexpected sight. People! There must have been about a dozen of them! After some discussion we figured they must be from the commercial camp located a few kilometres back down the trail and were at the lake for the day. Sure enough, when we got to the lake we ran into some of them.

While the guys went fishing again, I had some lunch and packed up my gear. Jim had volunteered to help me back down the cliff as I had expressed concern about the adventure. When I was ready the two of them accompanied me around the lake and helped me down the cliff. They tied my rope and theirs together and then tied my pack on the end of my rope (we use ropes to put our food bags up the trees away from the bears). They slid the pack down the cliff with Andy guiding it and me climbing down. When I got to the bottom of the chain section I took the pack from Andy, untied the two ropes and Jim pulled theirs back up. I put my rope in the pack and got the whole thing on my back, said goodbye to Andy and waved to Jim, and gingerly made my way down the rest of the cliff via the route Jim had suggested.

From that point it was a straightforward hike to the trees where I met the horses the people at the lake had used. They were standing in the only shade available, waiting patiently for their riders.

In another few kilometres I met up with the owner of the outfitting business who was bringing supplies into his camp with his covered wagon pulled by draft horses. Most of the trails below tree line in this area are old logging roads, so a covered wagon is ideal for hauling supplies. In fact, the owner said the wagon saved him from using twenty packhorses and the subsequent environmental damage.

After my chat with the man and his two kids, I continued hiking. At the McPhail Creek crossing I found my old runners and socks still in the tree so got them on for the creek and river crossings. Then I changed back to my dry socks and hiking boots and in another hour I was back at my wee truck.

When I looked back at the date of the foregoing trip and made some calculations, I realized that I was fifty-seven years old at the time. What was I thinking? Isn't this rather old to be solo backpack hiking and climbing cliffs in the process? Actually, I wasn't thinking about my age, I was just thinking about following my dream and seeing Carnarvon Lake.

More Hiking Stories

The Five-Hour Flounder

Ross Lake - February 23, 1994

Somewhere west of Lake Louise, on the British Columbia side of the Great Divide, is Ross Lake. While I've been there in the summer during the days when that portion of Highway 1A was open to vehicles, I'd been in pursuit of Ross Lake in the winter several times without any luck. I once spent a day looking for the trail off the Lake O'Hara Fire Road and another day accessing it from the west end of Highway 1A, now I was trying to find it from Lake Louise.

I was looking for a trail that I thought was no longer maintained or marked and, as far as I knew, went from Lake Louise below the slopes of Mount Saint Piran and Mount Niblock, but not as low down as Highway 1A. I had seen where it came out at Ross Lake, but I wanted to find the end that started at Lake Louise.

So, here I was parked at the stables at Lake Louise, skiing along a marked cross-country ski trail. Normally this trail is groomed, but today it wasn't so I broke a new trail until I met up with a more recently groomed ski trail. I followed this groomed trail downhill looking for the old trail to Ross Lake until I reached Highway 1A. (At the time this section was closed in winter and used as a cross-country ski trail.) I knew I shouldn't be on Highway 1A and had missed the Ross Lake Trail, however, I followed the highway beyond the groomed section on an old ski track. It wasn't long before I was bored with this easy trail so I took a minute to consider my options.

Up there was the mountain, here was the highway and somewhere in between was the trail to Ross Lake. Since there wasn't a lot of in between area I decided to head straight up hill, breaking trail in the snow. Into the woods I wandered, making my way around trees and over deadfall until I found an old trail. Assuming this was the old Ross Lake Trail I followed it west.

It was slow going as the snow was deep, but it was a well-blazed trail so I didn't expect to have any problems. Unfortunately it ended up at Highway 1A! This was not according to the map. I decided to follow it back the way I came to see where I'd gone wrong and to see where it came out on the groomed ski trail. When I came to a small open spot with a bit of a view I stopped for lunch. Since it was a cold day (about -23 C) I put on my warm-up pants and my big duvet jacket and enjoyed my thermos of tea and a sandwich.

After lunch I started skiing again and in no time I lost the trail. I wandered all around looking for it to no avail, so I just kept skiing in the same direction and lo and behold I picked it up again. This happened twice! Then I ended up on Highway 1A—again, close to the groomed ski trail. Going back up the trail I had made I decided to head back to my truck in the stables parking lot and go home. Then I missed the turn off for the stables as I hadn't made a good note of where I'd come out! A handsome young man came out of the staff housing for the Chateau Lake Louise, so I asked him if he knew where the Ross Lake Trail was. Just as I asked him I looked over his shoulder and right behind him was a sign for the trail to Ross Lake! It wasn't an old trail after all. Oh well, I can't win them all.

It was late, so I went back to the truck and drove home. Next week Ross Lake Trail for sure.

Next week didn't happen. A Chinook blew in and made havoc of all that beautiful powder snow, so I didn't go. It wasn't until late spring that I got back; this time in hiking boots.

Lake Louise was full of tourists wandering around on the lake trail, taking pictures of themselves and the lake and the Chateau Lake Louise. When I left to hike to Ross Lake I only met one guy on a mountain bike and no one else until I arrived at the lake, and that was a young Japanese girl who was just leaving as I was arriving.

In retrospect, I am glad I didn't ski to the lake as the trail crossed several avalanche paths and in the late spring I had to walk across old snow that had slid down onto the trail. The trail is mostly in the trees, but I enjoy the forest, and obviously I enjoy an adventure!

Kootenay Park Rockwall Trails

Tumbling Creek - Wolverine Pass - Helmet Creek
Kootenay National Park, August 23-25, 1994.

The Paint Pots along Highway 93 South in Kootenay National Park is the trailhead for Tumbling Creek. The part of the trail that goes to the Paint Pots (there is ochre in the soil which the native peoples used as war paint) is busy with tourist traffic as it is very short. When you have a big backpack on you feel a little ridiculous until you pass the Paint Pots. However, in an hour and a half we were at the first creek crossing which has a swinging bridge with the odd missing board.

Taking pictures of others crossing the swinging bridge is part of the adventure. Lorraine Worbey and Angela Ovens were cautious, but Trish Jevne and I had done it two years before so were a little braver. Previously Trish and I had hiked into Floe Lake, over Numa and Tumbling Passes and hiked down Tumbling Creek. This year we were hiking up Tumbling Creek and coming down Helmet Creek. Betty Walker was coming with us on this trip as far as our lunch stop as she only had the day to hike and we were going for three days. The distance to Tumbling Falls was not clear in our minds, but we were hoping it would not be too far for a good lunch stop. Unfortunately, the trail went on and on and we got more and more hungry, so we gave up finding the falls for lunch and stopped at a good viewpoint.

This viewpoint gave us a look at the narrow Tumbling Creek valley with the peaks above and the alpine meadows above tree line.

After lunch we said our goodbyes to Betty and continued on up the valley. We were high above the creek, gaining altitude at every step. (It's 1800 feet (554 metres) from the parking lot to Tumbling Creek campsite.) Tumbling Falls was much further than anticipated so we were glad we had lunch when we did. It would have been a long way back for Betty. The falls are very spectacular and not far from the campsite. The narrow, little bridge over the canyon just before the campground was exciting and a great photo opportunity. Trish and I had stayed at this campsite two years ago.

The campground had lots of campers, but there was room for our two tents. They were small enough to fit on one tent site and we had an excellent view of Tumbling Glacier in the distance.

"The Rockwall is composed of a dark grey Cambrian limestone and its east-facing cliffs form the backbone of the Vermilion Range for a stretch of nearly 40 kilometres." (Patton & Robinson 1978) It literally looks like a big rock wall. Floe Glacier and Tumbling Glacier drape themselves over the wall creating glacial silt ponds and Floe Lake.

In 1969 I had hiked and camped at Floe Lake with some hostel friends. In those days Floe Glacier came right into the lake and ice floes would break off the glacier and float in the lake. Two years ago when Trish and I visited the lake, we could see that the glacier had receded back into the moraines and rock and was no longer in the lake. I took a picture of the glacier in 1969 and another one in 1992. About 1971 I had also backpacked up Helmet Creek and over the route we were doing, but in reverse. It was high time I saw it all again!

From our campsite the next morning we continued our hike uphill to the meadows below the Rockwall and over to Wolverine Pass (on the boundary of Kootenay National Park and the British Columbia forest reserve) and looked west into the interior of British Columbia. The Rockwall Trail is a popular hike since it is very spectacular, so it was easy to find someone to take a group picture of the four of us on Wolverine Pass. Four cameras, four pictures.

Three middle aged ladies and one young girl in her twenties. We never seem to find other middle-aged ladies backpacking! Where are they? We can't possibly be crazy; this scenery is too good to miss, even the second time around! Alpine meadows, up and down ridges and all those marvellous views of the Rockwall; it really is a paradise.

From Rockwall Pass we dropped down to a creek that flows from one of the silt-laden lakes below the glacier, and met up with the trail crew building bridges and a trail through the moraines. Hiking uphill again, we continued over the shoulder of a ridge coming off the Rockwall and down, down, down to Helmet Creek. Picking berries along the way and finally seeing the spectacular Helmet Falls (1170 feet/360 metres), coming in two cascades down the huge cliff that forms part of the Rockwall.

At the bottom of the trail is another backcountry campground and we were not long in finding a suitable spot, getting our two tents up and finding shelter from the light rain that had started to fall. We found a kitchen spot among a thick grove of trees and it was no time before we had tea and supper brewing.

Settling in and getting dinner ready is always a fun occasion. This campsite was more like true backcountry camping. No picnic table here like at Tumbling Creek campsite. There were fire pits so Trish did her usual and in between showers we enjoyed the fire.

The following morning the other girls went off to the base of Helmet Falls, while I moseyed around the campsite and enjoyed the view of the falls from the creek. The morning is when the sun is directly lighting the waterfall and the view from the campsite, with the moss-lined creek in the foreground and the waterfall cascading in the background is breathtaking.

Once the girls returned, we packed up our camp and headed down Helmet Creek. This trail is not nearly as steep as Tumbling Creek, but it is nevertheless very nice with some good views of the narrow Helmet Creek valley. The trail meets up with the Tumbling Creek Trail and goes back to the Paint Pots.

A wonderful three day hike and highly recommended.

Sheep River Valley

Journal Entries

Sandy McNabb Campground

Kananaskis Country, Thursday, May 17, 2001. Sunny, warm, chilly periods.

After devotions, breakfast and a phone call, I finished packing the van, said goodbye to the cats and took off. First stop was the post office; second was Bragg Creek Village where I picked up a few groceries. As I was driving I realized I was short on food even though the cooler was full. When I arrived at Turner Valley I got gas, then on to the campground. Had a nice chat with the campground hosts, registered and had lunch. I should have had a rest as I was tired, but no, I took off for a hike right from the campground. I think I was on one of the cross-country ski trails. It was very pleasant with lovely views on the south part of the loop. 1.5 hours.

When I returned I laid down in the van and had a nice rest. As it was a bit cool, I think I would have slept if I had not had the back door open, but the view through it of the forest is peaceful. Read a little then got the Coleman stove out and food items and had a nice supper. Washed dishes, organized my van for the night and read while waiting for Sue to arrive.

The campground is starting to fill tonight. I'm impressed with the number of people who have arrived and are still coming in. The family next to me had their ghetto blaster going and I prayed to have it turned off or turned down and a few minutes later it was off.

While en route here I saw nine sheep at my house, four Canada geese, two goldeneye ducks and one violet on my walk.

Sue finally arrived, I had gone walking to the phone booth about 9:00 p.m. to call her and hadn't gone too far when she came rolling along in her dad's camperized bus. She had been parked at the equestrian campground and gone walking her dogs. I had expected we would do that together. She cooked her haphazard dinner and we chatted; dogs underfoot.

Sandy McNabb Campground

Kananaskis Country, Friday, May 18, 2001 Sunny

Here it is 8:45 a.m. and Sue has been gone for over an hour, walking her dogs I expect. No explanation, just gone! Camper and all. I've had my breakfast and am physically ready to go hiking. I am wondering what the scenario is going to be.

Sue finally came back and all turned out well. I asked what she had in mind for the weekend and she told me Dyson Falls and as far as the bridge over the Upper Sheep River was what she would like to do. So, while she had breakfast I walked the interpretive trail, came back and put a lunch together and we drove down to Indian Oils and hiked the 4.4 km to Dyson Falls. About half way there I thought she was going to can out as she sat down and said that was as far as she was going. I explained the trail to her and she continued. (We'd already done the major uphill.) The falls were looking really nice so we ate lunch with a view of the falls. There was still a fair bit of ice on the creek in the shady spots. It was a nice hike. We took her dog Alaska, but left Spook, who is in bad health, in her camper bus. We got back to the campsite about 4:00 p.m.

We saw sixteen sheep at Bighorn Lookout and lots of crocuses on the hike and a few three-flowered avens at the falls.

It was a mixture of sun and cloud and wind all day, but the wind has died down tonight. I had a couple of cups of tea when we got back and then made supper. Sue and I both had pork chops, so I did the sliced potatoes, carrots and onions in tinfoil on the fire and we barbequed the pork chops on the fire too.

I'm now packed up and sitting by the fire and Sue has gone off in her bus to walk the dogs somewhere one last time. I think she likes to go off by herself. In some ways she resents other campers, whereas I enjoy seeing them enjoying themselves—although I don't like ghetto blasters. In the end it's been a good day.

Sandy McNabb Campground

Kananaskis Country, Saturday, May 19, 2001, Sun, cloud, snow, wind.

I slept in until 8:00 a.m. today. Sue didn't show signs until 9:00 and then she drove off without a word and disappeared until after 11:00 a.m. I had a nice breakfast at the picnic table and then walked the interpretive trail in the opposite direction to yesterday. It started to rain on my way back and looked ominous to the west the whole time. When I got to the campsite Sue still wasn't back and, frankly, I am really ticked off. She asked me to go camping with her and then she disappears for hours without a word. I was seething by the time she returned. I sat in my van and was reading as it was raining. She opened the van door and said she was leaving and returned the pack I had loaned her. She did not sound happy and I didn't say much and off she went.

Shortly after that the rain quit and the sun came out, so I took off in the van for a trail—any trail. Just get me hiking! I stopped at Foran Grade trailhead and sat in the van and had lunch and watched hikers getting ready and taking off. Then I took off too, up Foran Grade Trail. The sun was beautiful and a warm Chinook wind was blowing; as I got higher on the ridge a north wind swooped down and chased the Chinook away. Its wind was so biting that I had to stop and put on my jacket, wool hat and mitts. Six horses with riders passed me as I started on the downward bit. It took me one hour and 25 minutes, to Windy Point Pass and 25 minutes down Windy Point Trail to the road. I crossed the road and took Sheep Trail back to Foran Grade trailhead parking.

Along Sheep Trail I saw one Canada goose that honked until I was past her. I saw several flowers throughout the hike: one crocus, shooting stars, squat dandelions, kinnikinnick, and strawberry blossoms.

Coming down Windy Point Trail it started to snow in little round balls. That changed to wet flakes and got heavier and heavier until visibility was poor as I tried to look down the steep slope to the Sheep River. What I could see is amazing. I'd like to see it on a clear day. When I got to the van I shook the snow off me and took off my wet anorak and drove back to the campsite. Almost the first thing I noticed was the dog chain around the tree that Sue had forgotten was missing. I assume she came back for it. I had planned to take it to her.

I climbed into the back of the van and made tea on my backpacking stove. When I arrived at the campsite the sun came out and the snow started melting off the trees and everything was wet. I'm letting it dry a bit before I venture out.

Now that I'm free to do what I want and not waste precious hours waiting on Sue, I'll get my map out and plan the next two days.

10:25 p.m.: cooked some of my dinner over the fire and some on the Coleman. After cleaning up I sat by the fire, feeding it and reading. The whole time I could hear some campers yelling and screaming in Loop A (I'm in Loop B). Some R.C.M.P. came to visit the people in the site across from me and I asked them to stop over there and tone them down. Nothing changed. Just before dark I took the slops to the toilet and the garbage to the dumpster and then walked around Loop B. Got settled in. I think it's going to be a cold night.

I sure enjoyed that hike today.

Sandy McNabb Campground

Kananaskis Country, Sunday, May 20, 2001. Sunny, warm, cool wind.

It was really cold last night and a lady at church told me she had icicles in her garden. I drove into Turner Valley and looked for a church about 10:00 a.m. I found one in Black Diamond (3 km further) with people going in! So, I did too. It was a good service and good preaching. I left right after the service and drove back to Kananaskis and to Indian Oils day use/trailhead.

I cooked up a hearty lunch of beans, egg, raw carrots, cookies and Postum. I also talked to a couple looking at the trail map. Trail counseling! Then I walked down to the bridge over Tiger Jaw Falls and took the Sheep Trail west. I have never been on that bit before and it intrigued me when Sue and I went the other way to Dyson Falls. I walked all the way to Junction Creek, which is where any semblance of a trail stops. I sat on my pack on a rock overlooking the creek, ate my apple and had a drink of water. It was very peaceful. I saw two horses with riders go by on Junction Creek Trail on the other side of the creek.

En route, near the beginning of the trail I passed three people—two girls and a guy. The guy was pushing a baby in a Burley. I'd seen the track and suspected I'd see them. They had not gone far. It was a pleasant 4.5 km walk to Junction Creek. I could hear the highway across the river some of the time. On the way back there was a long stretch where I could hear a ghetto blaster thumping away. How rude. I got back to my van at 4:40 p.m.

When I got back to the campsite a truck was parked at my pull-thru, but they quickly left. I found my picnic tablecloth on the ground, blown off the table because someone had stolen my clips that hold it on. That sure made me mad—such a petty crime. I put the cloth back on the table and have held it down with rocks on the corners. Then I made dinner. I've been using my big billy to heat dish water over the fire which works very well. I used the last of my wood to build the fire. It was just enough to heat the water. I haven't seen the campground hosts cruising around with firewood tonight.

The people across the way have had their stereo going and are now listening to a game on the radio and the cute kids next door are blowing whistles. There seems to be more people noise tonight, but not the screaming like last night. Today I saw eight geese on my way to and from Black Diamond and two on my way back from Indian Oils.

To get away from the noise I went for a walk at eight o'clock down to the picnic site by the river. I started on the road and then found a trail. I wandered along another trail by the river and saw what I think was a sandpiper. On my way back I saw a whitetail deer across the river in a bit of meadow. I also found the section of the Sheep Trail that crosses the river. I picked up a horse trail on the way back uphill and got back to the campsite at 9:25 p.m.—a longer walk than I anticipated. Saw about four people, plus a truckload of kids with a massive dog. Down by the river there is a wonderful view of the hills and cliffs across the river and the big, snowy mountains peaking through the hills—very quiet there and so restful.

Sandy McNabb Campground to Exshaw

Monday, May 21, 2001 Sunny and Hot!

Gone is the rain and snow, welcome to summer sunshine. Oh joy! I slept in until 8:40 a.m. and awoke feeling good. Had breakfast at the picnic table and packed up everything for the trip home. Drove to Gorge Creek Trail road; first stopping to read the sign about Nash Meadow at the former Bighorn Ranger Station. I had not gone far up Gorge Creek Trail when I saw two vehicles stopped and noticed they were watching a chubby cinnamon bear. I didn't stop more than a few seconds as the road is narrow with no shoulder. I stopped at Gorge Creek trailhead to use the biffy and talked to some hikers, then drove on to Ware Creek trailhead.

From here I hiked Link Trail to Ware Creek Trail and along it to Death Valley Trail. After hiking about 1.5 hours I saw two people sitting in an aspen meadow with their backs to me. I soon recognized them as Tony and Gillean Daffern (my publishers), so I joined them for lunch and walked with them as they were going my way. I kept thinking how rare for the two experts on Kananaskis (Gill and me) to meet on a trail, albeit in Kananaskis. They were looking for the Muriel Dixon native gravesite and cross. They did find it. It was up on a meadowed hill with a panoramic view of the surrounding hills.

We lounged around by the grave and I gave up going the extra kilometre to Windy Point Trail junction as I was a bit tired. I'd now gone 7.5 km. Gill took multiple pictures, including a couple of just me. A whole flock of tree swallows swooped and spun over our heads. At one point we saw two horse riders down on the Death Valley Trail going onto 9999 Trail. The latter is named after John Ware's horse brand and Ware Creek and trail are named after him. Ware was a black cowboy who escaped slavery in the U.S. in the 1800s. He was amazingly strong and a great rider. He has been immortalized in Alberta history.

Along the trails I saw robins, a black and white bird that I haven't been able to identify, shooting stars, stubby dandelions, buttercups, scorpion weed, chickweed, violets, three-flowered avens, and strawberry blossoms. There were lots of dead leaves crunching under my feet along the trail as there are golden aspen trees in this area. The various meadows and hill views were prolific. There were also a few creek fords, but I never got my feet wet, although Gill did when she went to check out a bit of trail.

Gill and Tony said their goodbyes (it was such a treat to meet and hike with them) and I plodded on the last bit that included more creek crossings, but no wet feet.

I got back to the van really tired. I took my time changing my boots. The van was so warm that the hand washing water I keep in a margarine container was warm, so I got a good hand wash, and the outhouse was handy to dump my slops. I drove to Humpty's Restaurant at the PetroCanada station on Highway One for supper. I didn't have much food left at home and I was starved and exhausted after my 15 km hike.

I arrived home just after 9:00 p.m. and, after unloading the van and patting the cats, I took my messages off the answering machine. Sue had called today, so I called her back while I ran a tub bath. I found out that when Sue left me Saturday she went somewhere until the rain quit, then she hiked the Sandy McNabb Interpretive Trail and then went down the valley to Bluerock. She did not return until close to 3:00 p.m. when it was snowing heavily because she said she passed my van at Foran Grade trailhead and saw it had a pile of snow on it!

Later, as I lay in my bathtub and mulled things over I realized I'd been had. No more camping with Sue. It was a blessing to have met up with Gillian and Tony and a beautiful weekend of hiking in the Sheep Valley.

Blitzing the Smith-D

Beautiful weather and what could be finer than a day off in Kananaskis Country hiking the side valleys off the Smith-Dorrien/Spray Trail road.

Buller Creek

Yes, another wonderful day in the Canadian Rockies and up Buller Creek it was. No, not to South Buller Pass, this time it was to finally see the north fork of Buller Creek. At the third bridge on the trail turn left on a smaller trail. It varies from well defined to faint, but it got me there. This was a solo hike over rock and meadows, snow and waterfalls. They were all there to be enjoyed. I had just got out into the open meadow when thunder threatened, but I continued on. When I finally got to the head of the valley and was longingly looking at North Buller Pass the thunder really yelled at me. I beat a hasty retreat to some trees to eat my lunch—none of that little pointy-head sticking above the meadows for me.

This is an amazing valley with exciting rock formations and a great waterfall. This is the route of the original pack trail that Alvin Guinn cut in the 1930s. There are still some tipi poles left to see if you get on the right trail. I didn't see anyone in the north fork, but four people wandered by me on the main trail, although they never saw me off in the woods having a rest. Six hours later I was back at the van—tired and happy.

Headwall Lakes to Chester Lake

Somebody finally saw my ad in the ACC *Blizzard* newsletter about wanting hiking companions on Mondays and Tuesdays.

A cool and cloudy day greeted Bill and Lucille Pulliam, Ray Kodama and Ruthie as they parked at the Chester Lake parking lot and headed off to the Headwall Creek valley. We trekked our way through the cross-country ski trails to Headwall Creek and trundled up the undesignated trail and first headwall to the first Headwall Lake. Pretty amazing. It is absolutely wonderful with yellow buttercups everywhere. On to the second Headwall Lake via rock and snow and from there we followed the small streams with their bit of greenery, crossing snow patches and wet spots to the base of the Headwall-Chester Col. The cornice looked formidable, but Ray led us up the right hand side and we arrived on the col in due course to enjoy the awesome scenery while eating lunch.

The steep scree and snow slope on the Chester Lake side of the col was a great challenge to Bill and Lucille who had never in their wildest dreams done anything like this. It was soon apparent they needed help so Ruthie and Ray came to the rescue. Ray helped Bill and Ruthie grabbed Lucille's hand and hung on for dear life. Four times she fell flat on her back on the snow and four times Ruthie held on tight. Once Ruthie looked at her own boots and wondered who was holding them! Once at the bottom Bill and Lucille looked up and said, "Our children will never believe this!"

Scrambling over rocks and snow, lolling in a little meadow with an emerald green stream running through it added to the idyllic scene. Those big peaks all around were awesome and a long way from Delaware, U.S.A. and Surrey, B.C. Chester Lake and its meadows were superb and enthralled Lucille especially.

Nine hours later we arrived back at the parking lot. Exhausted, but happy. Chinese food in Canmore sounded great and tasted marvellous.

Commonwealth - Smuts Pass

The next week it was Commonwealth Creek enticing us onward. This time Lorraine Worbey and Sherri LaFreniere joined Bill, Lucille and Ruthie for another nine-hour rhapsody.

The waterfall ensured we were following Gillean Daffern's directions and from there on the route finding was easy. The flowers and meandering creek were marvellous. No bears were sighted in the cow parsnip and forget-me-not meadows. The grunt up Smuts Pass was broken up with a lunch break. Once at the pass, Smuts Lake was a gem to behold. Down the pass and across the meadows and rocks and then more uphill past a beautiful waterfall and Ice Lake—so Gillean calls it—and on to High Col.

Wowee!! The view of the mountains is outstanding. The flowers are amazing, snow patches are everywhere and there is Birdwood Pass looking ever so inviting! Another day Ruthie. It was so wonderful we spent an hour lolling on the col and just enjoying everything. Even Kodak benefited from the view. All too soon we had to head back.

Black Prince Lake

A skip and a jump and we were down the interpretive trail to Warspite Lake and ready for the real adventure. Around the lake and through the trees Bill, Lucille, Ray and Ruthie did go. Up the marvellous, flowered hillside near the cascading waterfall we trudged. Ruthie saw wet bear droppings and blithely said it was old, knowing full well it was only a couple of hours old. (Why worry people unduly.) Yodeling is a good vocalization in bear country so Ruthie did her bit. Up and up that hillside with the most outstanding columbine flowers we'd ever seen—hundreds of them. Marvellous waterfall. Finally we reached the top and entered the high meadows and followed the meandering stream to the head of the valley. Lunch break by the stream, then up the rock dam that keeps Black Prince Lake from flushing down the valley. The lake still had ice on it and lots of melting snow patches making it one lake and not the three the map shows. A walk along the ridge revealed Warspite Lake below and marvellous mountain views. After a rest on top, Lucille and Ruthie literally cooled their heels in a snow patch.

It's great having the time to loll in the meadows and on the ridges to enjoy the views, the flowers and our lunches. How many hours was this one Lucille?

Sparrowhawk Tarns

Just the three of us: Bill, Lucille and Ruthie. Once more we followed Gillean's directions and found a nice trail that took us to tree line where we followed our noses. Read's Tower looked inviting. Mount Sparrowhawk looked inviting. We, however, were headed for the tarns. Up the rockslide, up meadows and rocks, followed by lunch under the last trees in the meadows while the thunder echoed overhead. We took a safety break against a rocky overhang where we waited for the thunder to pass. It didn't really rain on us, just threatened. Finally it seemed safe to continue, so on we trudged. Over the rocks, up the rocks, around the tarns and waterfalls, around the marvellous meadow of saxifrage and past gorgeous little yellow buttercups until we finally reached the head of the valley and the last tarn. Wonderful! Cascading waterfalls off Mount Bogart echoing amongst the rocks. It was too idyllic for words. We had another long loll in the meadow at the last tarn, soaking up the atmosphere of the high mountain valley. It was with great reluctance we headed back.

Was that another nine hour day Lucille?

Lucille and Bill Pulliam overlooking Sparrowhawk Tarns, 1997.

We've started a trend. After our first group hike we went for Chinese dinner in Canmore, then after the second one we had spaghetti dinner at Bill and Lucille's house in Canmore, and then the trend started: picnic suppers at a Kananaskis picnic site. Buller Mountain overlooking Buller Pond and then Driftwood day use overlooking Spray Lakes Reservoir and we're planning another one somewhere for the next hike. The picnic site has to have fire pits and we bring our firewood. There's nothing quite like Valbella's bratwurst done over an open fire! It makes a wonderful ending to a day in the mountains.

Tryst Lake for Supper

Life in an information centre in Kananaskis Country means you spend hours telling hundreds of people where to go hiking, picnicking and camping. If you don't get out and do some of these activities yourself you feel cheated. When Labour Day dawned bright and sunny I took a change of clothes and my hiking boots to work. When my shift ended I changed into my hiking clothes and drove down the Kananaskis Valley, first stopping in Kananaskis Village to buy a picnic supper at the deli in The Lodge at Kananaskis. The next stop was the Mount Shark Road and a small parking spot not far from Mount Engadine Lodge. The parking spot was almost full of cars, but as I was putting on my hiking boots a group of hikers started trickling in after their day hiking up Commonwealth Creek. As I headed out on the trail at 5:03 p.m. I passed the last of the group and then the area was all mine.

A half hour of easy walking took me to the rock cairn in which someone had stuck several long sticks with a bit of flagging tape that marks the turn off for Tryst Lake. The trail up to the lake was easy to find, but the scramble up that 845 feet (260 meters) was a push. It was a good thing I'd had that can of Sprite with its sugar content—it kept me going.

In its lower elevations Tryst Creek has lots of moss and is really pretty. All of the elevation gain happens in one fell swoop, so it's up, up, up. The route is through a narrow little gully with some awesome views across the Smith-Dorrien valley and occasional glimpses of Mount Engadine Lodge. There are enough open spots to keep one's interest. Just after the trail leveled out, I arrived at the lake; a truly spectacular setting. The Fist Mountain rises above the lake and the surrounding rock of the cirque makes it a marvellous scene. The meadows were inviting me to pitch my little tent. Unfortunately, this is inside Peter Lougheed Provincial Park and the side valleys in the park along the Smith-Dorrien/Spray Trail road are closed to backcountry campers, so future plans were not allowed.

After eating my delicious picnic supper in the last of the sun, I walked around the lake and up into the head of the valley where I could see its unique dip. Walking back around the other side of the lake allowed me to identify the seven Coots in the lake. They sure added to the peaceful setting. An hour after arriving I reluctantly left this idyllic place. The view going back down Tryst Creek is outstanding. A few black currants were a welcome addition to my supper. In just over an hour I was back at the parking spot.

I highly recommend going out for supper.

Is it Scree or is it Moraine?

Two steps up, one step down; two steps up, one step down. Is this scree or is it moraine? We struggle up the steep slope. Is this a vain attempt to get into the cirque or will we really reach our goal? Is it all words and sweat or are we making progress? How do you describe movable scree? As I look at Running Rain Lake below us I realize we are making progress, but it is such a struggle. I am getting exhausted.

How do you find words to describe this difficult scree or to describe the beautiful wildflowers growing in the scree? Yellow columbine, blue forget-me-nots, white camas with yellow centres, purple penstemon, Indian paintbrush, I search valiantly for the words to describe them all. Bell shaped penstemon, drooping heads of the columbine, white camas reaching to the sky are words, but without actually seeing these beautiful flowers do you know what they look like? Do I have to get out my flower book and quote from it for the description? Will those words paint a picture of the flowers for you?

I think these thoughts about the flowers, but then I am back struggling in the scree and the flowers are fewer the higher I go, but the purple penstemon still clutch to little bits of soil in the rocks and their mats of colour brighten the slope. Finally Krystyna Jahns and I reach the cirque and are greeted by the grey rubble of the rock.

We had hoped to find a little lake, but alas we are disappointed. Is it still scree or is it now moraine? That looks like a glacial hole in the rubble of rock. If it's glacial, it must be moraine.

What is scree and what is moraine you ask? Scree is loose rocks, usually on a steep mountain slope, and moraine is compacted rocks that are pushed by glaciers as they work their way downhill. Moraine usually becomes a steep sided ridge, but not always. We are standing on such a ridge with patches of purple penstemon being the only colour. The steep cliffs above us are just as grey as the moraine.

I stand on the edge of the cirque and look at Mist Mountain across the valley. Its brown variegated contours shine in the sun and give me a warm feeling of awe. Gazing at Running Rain Lake below surrounded by green meadows is also delightful. It looks so small from this height. I'm filled with joy because the hot struggle was worth the effort.

Mount Joffre

Alberta was celebrating its centennial in many different ways in 2005. Since I had married Kananaskis in 1972 I had two things I wanted to do for my part in the celebration. One was to climb Mount Joffre, the highest peak in Kananaskis Country at 11316 feet (3450 meters), and the other was to do the traverse hike of Mount Allan, the highest maintained trail in Canada at 9249 feet (2819 meters).

During the winter I asked Lloyd "Kiwi" Gallagher, a professional guide and former Kananaskis Country employee, if he would take me up Mount Joffre. In early July he contacted me to say that George Field was organizing the past rangers and current conservation officers to climb the peak in small groups over a one-week period to celebrate the centennial. Kiwi said he had three days off from his guiding job with the cadets and we could go with George in the first group.

George had arranged for us to be taken by boat close to the Hidden Lake Trail and from there we hiked up to the Aster Lake conservation officers' cabin where we stayed the night. We were a group of six and when a friend showed up in the rain we squeezed him into the tiny cabin. The camaraderie was excellent.

The following morning we were up at 4:30 a.m. and starting out at 5:30 a.m. for the mountain. We hiked up to Aster Lake, working our way around the bushes and little cliffs by the lake and along a stretch of moraine and snow to a point where we put on our crampons and tied into the climbing rope. Once into softer snow we took off the crampons and continued our way uphill. Kiwi was leading me, and the others were divided into two ropes. At one point we stopped for a lunch break. The others soon passed us and cut steps into the steeper section of the mountain. At 10,750 feet (3307.6 metres) we were engulfed in a snowstorm and I ran out of gas. I told Kiwi I couldn't go any further, but asked him to tie me into the mountain and to go ahead. As a guide he couldn't do that and was shocked that I'd asked. While he had been on the summit four times I felt it was a big disappointment for him not to make it for the centennial climb, but he never let on. He organized our gear and we went back down arriving at the cabin 14 hours after we had started out.

When the others returned they kept telling me how proud they were that I had got as high as I did. I expected to get to the summit, but they didn't think I would make it so high. I was 68 years old and Kiwi was 66 years old. Kiwi continued to guide for a couple more years, but I decided it was my last big mountain.

Alex Baradoy, Christine Scotland, Ed Kujak, Ruthie and George Field in front of the Aster Lake Conservation Officers' Cabin, Kananaskis Country, 2005. Photo: Lloyd Gallagher.

The following day on our way back from the cabin to the trailhead we met the next group of conservation officers at Hidden Lake on their way in for their part in the centennial climbing week.

Mount Allan

It was 35 years since I first hiked the whole traverse over Mount Allan. One time when I was part way up the mountain I had a yearning to do this traverse again. Just before the first of September I told my hiking group that I wanted to do the traverse of Mount Allan on the Centennial Trail for the Alberta 2005 centennial. I said it was 18 km long and 1231 meters elevation gain. Would they be interested? Several of them said yes.

On September second a group of eleven of us did the traverse from Ribbon Creek to Pigeon Mountain. It was actually 1369 meters elevation gain. We had beautiful weather and everyone made it the whole way. It took 12 hours and I was very proud of them. Not a whiner in the bunch.

Lynda Beyer Remembers

We were hiking Mount Allan's Centennial Trail. It had been a long but spectacular hike up until this point. Earlier in the afternoon some of us had called home on our cell phones to let family members know we would be home around 5:00 p.m. Donna Iddings borrowed my phone to call her husband Roger. As the Iddings do not have an answering machine she couldn't leave a message but Roger would have my cell number as they had *call display*. It was now around 9:00 p.m. and the wind had picked up and the sky had darkened with storm clouds and night was approaching. The trees started swaying dangerously and we could hear the rumble of thunder in the distance. We tried to pick up the pace but our legs were tired from the long hike. Most of us had run out of food and water a couple hours ago. The hike was taking longer than expected.

Donna, Anna and Krystyna broke from the group at a faster pace. It didn't take long before they were out of sight. We weren't worried as the three ladies were all experienced hikers. We trudged on as the thunder moved closer and large drops of rain started to fall. After a wet and windy half hour we finally came to the last bit of trail. There was a fork and Ruthie guided us expertly on the right path to our cars, five minutes ahead. We reached our cars just before 10:00 p.m. in the gathering darkness, but it didn't take long to realize the three ladies who had forged ahead were nowhere in sight. They must have taken the wrong path at the fork. Hopefully it wouldn't take them long before they realized their mistake. In the meantime, some of us went back to the Ribbon Creek parking lot to pick up the vehicles we had used to transport ourselves to the trailhead while Ruthie waited for the women. I was worried as the storm was not abating, it was dark and I knew they were tired. Hopefully they would have found the right trail and their ride home before we returned to the trail end parking lot.

I was thinking these thoughts and sending up a prayer when my cell phone rang.

This is something that doesn't happen often as only my family members have my number. I had already called home from the trail end parking lot to let my kids know I was okay. They had been worried and were relieved to hear my voice. It was now 10:30 p.m. I answered the call and a male voice hollered into the phone "Where's my wife?" I was a little slow at recognizing who was on the other end and so asked, "Who is this?" "This is Roger and where's my wife!"

Roger is a no nonsense businessman and I could tell by the tone of his voice he was very concerned and not a happy man. I wasn't sure how to answer Roger's question, as I really didn't know exactly where his wife was. She was very likely waiting for me at the trail end parking lot. On the other hand, she could still be out on some trail in this storm. I didn't want to worry Roger with this last thought so I tried to sooth him by answering "She is most likely waiting for me at the end of the trail where we parked the cars. The hike took much longer than anticipated but we should be home within the hour." At this Roger explained that it was Donna's birthday (none of us knew this) and he had prepared a dinner for her and had been waiting for several hours for her to come home. I remembered that the last time we had had cell phone contact was in the afternoon, so I felt terrible and worried all the more about where Donna might be.

After many prayers were sent up, we arrived back at the end of the trail where the others were waiting. The rain had dissipated and the storm was moving on. As I turned into the parking lot, in the headlights of my van I saw the three ladies, looking tired and wet but safe. Praise God!!

The moral of this story is not to get too far ahead of your trusty hiking leader, especially if you don't know the trail or if it is already dark and stormy. Better to stay with the group. All in all it had been quite an adventure.

Rini Boers on the
summit of Mount Allan,
Kananaskis Country, 1970.

Chapter 6

Getting Personal

Ruthie writing her trail guide in Kananaskis, 1977. Photo: Jan Boschman.

Writing Books

*I*t wasn't my plan, or even a thought, to write a book, however, life is full of adventures.

After a year running the Ribbon Creek Hostel in Kananaskis Country I realized I couldn't live on my honorarium of 75 dollars a month. (When I quit after 8.5 years it was 215 dollars a month.) The only possible place of employment in Kananaskis at that time (1973) was the University of Calgary's field station at Barrier Lake, 16 km north of the hostel. I went there and asked for a job that I could do between the hours of 10:00 a.m. and 5:00 p.m.—the hours the hostel was closed during the day. I fully expected to be washing floors; however, I was given the job of organizing their technical library.

I did that for some months when one day while having coffee with the cook, Pearl Williams, and the director's assistant, Linda Jones, I mentioned that I'd read every English monarch's biography from Henry VIII to George V. Linda piped up that they needed someone to write the human history of the Kananaskis Valley for the *Man and the Biosphere – Kananaskis Pilot Study* project.

Jon Brehaut, who was working on his master's degree, did a bit on the outside views of the times, but I was left to do the rest. I was really out of my depth, but that turned out to be beneficial as it enabled me to flounder around and learn how to research and write—two activities for which I had no experience or education.

By the time my chapter was finished there was a lot of publicity surrounding the creation of Kananaskis Country. I thought the public would be interested in knowing the history of the Kananaskis Valley, so I approached Dr. Gordon Hodgson, director of the field station, and convinced him to fund me to expand the history into book form for the general public. Thus, in 1978 my book *The Valley of Rumours...the Kananaskis* was completed.

At the same time I was working on that book I was also hiking and cross-country skiing and writing up trail descriptions for another book. I finished this little book, *The Kananaskis Valley Hikers and X-C Skiers Guide*, a little before I'd finished the history book.

Once the guide book was finished I approached Bart Robinson and Brian Patton (the authors of the first Canadian Rockies Trail Guide) about having them publish it through their Devils Head Press. Brian said they were not interested, but why didn't I publish it myself? He offered to give me a list of all their good retail outlets, which he did, as well as advice on getting it printed. Don't get it printed in Alberta he said as it costs four times the price of printing in Manitoba or Ontario.

My brother-in-law, Stuart Cummings, in Sioux Lookout, Ontario, was in the printing business at the time and he put me onto Bilko Printing in Kenora, Ontario, and I contracted them to do the printing. At a quarter of the price of an Alberta quote!

In the meantime, the University of Alberta Press, who Dr. Hodgson had contacted about publishing my Kananaskis history book, said it would be about three years before they would be able to get it out. He wanted the book out sooner because of the high profile of Kananaskis Country at the time. By then my trail guide was published so I suggested that I could get the book out sooner through the little company I'd formed called Ribbon Creek Publishing Company. All I needed was the money.

The money, ah yes. I didn't have any. To get the money to print the trail guide I wrote Premier Peter Lougheed and told him what I did for a living, how much money I didn't have and how important Kananaskis Country was and could I borrow some money from the government to print my book? Mr. Lougheed forwarded my letter to the Alberta Opportunity Company that had just been formed. I subsequently received a visit at the hostel from a gentleman with that company. He must have thought I was a good bet because the company loaned me the money and I just had to repay it on a per book sold basis. When the Alberta Opportunity Company came out with their first newsletter I was interviewed for the front page story.

"Ruthie Writes about History and Trails in the Kananaskis Valley"

Published and written by the Alberta Opportunity Company in their newsletter Success Stories first edition c. 1978

"The first night that she trekked out under the stars in the Rocky Mountains Charlotte "Ruthie" Oltmann knew she belonged there. Today, some eight years later, she is a living legend in the Kananaskis Valley and has written a couple of books about the area.

Her history of the region entitled "The Valley of Rumours...the Kananaskis" and "The Kananaskis Valley Hikers' and Cross Country Skiers' Guide" (AOC financed) have made author publisher "Ruthie" the reigning authority on the Valley.

Both books were published in 1978 after four years of exhaustive research. Oltmann hiked and skied every trail in the Valley, including one named after her, in putting together the Guide and spent hundreds of hours in various archives, libraries, museums and speaking with local inhabitants in piecing together the history of the Valley.

"In writing the books I was in the right place at the right time," she says, "I didn't have any research instruction so I learned as I went along."

After completing the text for her first book she went into hospital two days later. "My stomach reacted because I was so keyed up over finishing it", she recalls. "I almost quit the Guide twice but a friend kept me writing. It was a thrill to finally see it in print."

A publisher whom she approached recommended that she publish the books herself. Demonstrating resourcefulness, she selected a printer and distributed the books herself to retail outlets throughout Alberta. The Guide has now gone into its second printing and the history is selling steadily.

The Kananaskis Valley is located approximately 90 km west of Calgary in Kananaskis County. Snow-capped mountains, alpine meadows, clear bubbling streams, glacial lakes, evergreen forests and rolling foothills make up the scenery of the area. Kananaskis County is being developed as a year-round multi-use recreational area."

More Book Writing

After the Alberta Opportunity Company provided the funds to publish my trail guide I spoke with Dr. Hodgson of the Kananaskis field station and he had the University of Calgary make a similar loan arrangement for the history book. I had it printed at Bilko Printing as well. The university had never done a thing like that before.

Both books had two printings. The trail guide sold about 8,000 copies and the history something similar. I had my trail guide out one year before Gillean Daffern had her *Kananaskis Trail Guide* out. Because I was both the author and the publisher of these books I ended up making 40 per cent on each book, versus 10 per cent if I was just the author. This helped me out tremendously from a financial point of view; however, it also broadened my horizons by teaching me about the publishing and distribution business and introduced me to interesting and fascinating people. With the first year's proceeds I was able to buy a little truck and take a trip to Britain.

Once the second printing of the trail guide sold out I didn't bother reprinting it because I could see Gillean Daffern's book was filling that niche. Sometime later when the second printing of *The Valley of Rumours...the Kananaskis* was sold out and the stores were asking for more I realized it needed to be updated with the formation of Kananaskis Country in it. However, the stores were in a hurry for more books. I tried to contact the printing company to get more printed only to find they had changed hands three times and were no longer in business and no one knew where the plates were. The dye had been cast and I had to update it.

Prior to the last copy of the history being sold I had written the biography of Lizzie Rummel over the course of a year. When I finished it I sent it off to a publisher. They had it for a year and I hadn't heard from them. You can't send a manuscript to more than one publisher at a time. About then I met Eric and Patricia Holmgren who are historical writers, and explained what had happened. They said it was quite legitimate to write the publisher and ask after the status of the book. A month later I had my manuscript returned with an apology. They had lost it in their office and it took them a month to find it!

By that time I was working for Travel Alberta at the Barrier Lake Visitor Centre in Kananaskis Country and in 1983 was sent to Cold Lake, Alberta, to work in a visitor centre for the summer. While there I worked on making changes to my Lizzie Rummel book after my friend Dr. Floyd Snyder had made some helpful suggestions. While in Cold Lake I visited Maxine Hancock in Marwayne, a writer I'd taken a class from once, and she said "Don't give up on publishing it yourself. You have a good story." I had not wanted to publish it myself, but figured if there were no hitches and doors opened I'd look into it. In the end I did publish it and whenever I needed money I had it. That was the first printing of *Lizzie Rummel: Baroness of the Canadian Rockies*.

Back to the history book and its update. By this time Tony and Gillean Daffern were going strong with their publishing company Rocky Mountain Books. Since I had known them for some years I walked into their office one day and asked if they would be interested in doing a second printing of my Lizzie book and doing my new version of the history book. They said yes immediately. They got going on the Lizzie book and I started working on the history book update.

I was now working full time in the Barrier Lake Visitor Information Centre and the Canmore Travel Information Centre, so work on the book was a part time job. It took me four years to write because it took on a life of its own and got expanded into what became, essentially, a new book with a lot more data. Since I knew all of the former scientists from the University of Calgary's Barrier Lake field station I got some marvellous stories from them. The book came out in the summer of 1997 and is called *My Valley ◆ the Kananaskis.* Both my Lizzie book and this second Kananaskis book are still on the market.

Once that book was done I put together a family history of my father's side of the family with old photos and family reunion photos.

1997 was also the year my sister Nora Lea had an Oltmann family Christmas at her home near Sudbury, Ontario. When I went to the family Christmas I took along copies of my Kananaskis book and the family history for each of my siblings as a Christmas gift. Seven of the nine brothers and sisters were there. I had put each gift in a brown envelope with their names on it. As I handed each person their package I would not let them open them until everyone had theirs. When they did open them there was stunned silence. They had forgotten I'd mentioned in a Christmas letter that I was writing the book and they didn't know about the family history.

Backtracking once more to a little scenario. When I was almost finished my first history book, *The Valley of Rumours...the Kananaskis*, I could see the light at the end of the tunnel, so was working on it six days a week and working at the hostel seven days a week. Four days after the book went to the printer I ended up very sick and alone at the hostel. I had to drive the 16 km to the University of Calgary's field station to get help, trying not to throw up. Dennis Jaques drove me to the General Hospital in Calgary where I spent four days. The doctors couldn't find the source of the problem, but an English professor friend clued me in later saying it was probably stress from pushing myself.

Subsequently, when I finished my Lizzie book and mailed it off to the publisher, the one who lost it, I packed my gear and took off on a three-day solo backpack hike to Egypt Lake in Banff National Park. I walked out those stresses.

Sometime in 2004 Dene Cooper, who was heading up the writing of the Exshaw history book, asked me to interview people who lived or had lived in Exshaw to get their biographies for the book. This was a delightful project and I met many wonderful people who had some amazing stories to tell. I discovered there were a lot of very humble people living in Exshaw. That book came out in 2005 and is called *Exshaw the Heart of the Valley.*

Now we come to this book. Number five not counting the family history and the Exshaw book contribution.

I was retired, I had no plans to write another book and every time someone asked what I was writing I said, "I'm retired." Then Mark and Julie Kent gave me a beautiful iMac computer as they were upgrading. My old Mac was 12 years old and there was data on it I wanted to keep. I took it to a store in Calgary to have the data taken off and put on CDs. Unfortunately, the computer was too old and they couldn't do that. I brought the machine home, hooked it up again, and printed all the data I wanted. When I saw the number of stories I already had I got digging in my file cabinet and found more stories. I ended up with three thick file folders of stories. Vi Sandford said she could scan them onto a CD so I could use them. Once more the dye was cast and I started adding stories from my memory bank as well and, as they say, the rest is history.

Living with Pain

rowing up in a big family is a good way to get all the childhood diseases going around. In a family of nine children we were ensured that we got them all, including several of us getting scarlet fever during World War II. We were quarantined at the time and Daddy couldn't go back to piloting mail planes until we were better. Because he didn't get scarlet fever he had to nurse the rest of us. I was told that I was delirious for a week.

From the age of six onwards I did a number on my bones and have broken over two dozen by now. The first time I just fell off the verandah trying to catch a black cat and broke my arm. There could be a moral to that story. The second time I was thirteen and riding a friend's bicycle when I turned on gravel not knowing you don't do that. I broke the same arm and had to push the bike home with one hand.

When I went to Europe in 1968 I got sick in Spain and ended up in Geneva hospital for nine days with gastroenteritis and a bowel infection. By the time I got to the Rotterdam area, supposedly to have Christmas with my friends Tom and Jean Van Heijst, I was back in hospital again for eight days. By then my weight was down to 100 pounds. I don't know if that started it or not, but somewhere in the next several years I was having intestinal problems and was in pain almost every day. That went on for nine years before a doctor and I started to find a solution. It was another five or six years before I was better and discovered that I was lactose intolerant. There was a lot of pain over those fifteen years.

In 1985 thirty-five Alpine Club of Canada members hiked to Abbot Pass Hut from Lake O'Hara in celebration of Banff National Park's centennial. Unfortunately, I couldn't get up at four in the morning so missed climbing Mount Victoria, however, I did go with the group down the Lower Victoria Glacier through the Death Trap to Lake Louise. I was on Bernie Schiesser's rope along with others. One of the men was having a terrible time with his footing as he didn't have good boots or an ice axe. I was fine so I loaned him my ice axe and he did better. Banging my feet onto the glacier for traction didn't help my back. I did something to it and subsequently spent the next eight years in greater or lesser pain every day. One day a physiotherapist found the problem and pressed gently, but firmly, and pushed the bone back in place. Oh joy, I was free of pain. I walked around as if I was walking on glass I was so afraid of it going wrong again.

Then there was the time I took JT Gill cross-country skiing to Chester Lake and a bit beyond on a government workday. JT was new at skiing. When we got back down to the wide trail I told JT to go ahead and I'd meet him at the parking lot. He took off in a mad rush and I was giving chase when I fell on a rough corner. "Oooo, that felt a bit different," I thought, however, I got up and was off again. A month later I went to the doctor because something in my hip wasn't right. After an x-ray, bone scan, and a visit to the orthopedic surgeon it was determined I had a hip stress fracture. I spent a month and a half sitting on the couch waiting for that to heal – and read 15 books.

Two years before I retired as supervisor of visitor information in Kananaskis Country I took over the supervision of the Peter Lougheed Provincial Park Visitor Centre (I was still supervising the Barrier Lake Visitor Information Centre) and was setting up the gift shop displays to improve sales. I wanted to put a stand with a T-shirt on it onto a high ledge. I couldn't find a ladder or a solid chair, so I did what I should not have done; I stood on a wheeled, swivel chair on tile. I wasn't on the chair very long before I fell through the air with the greatest of ease, but unlike a trapeze artist I hit my back on a counter on the way down and landed on the floor on my side. I ended up going to Canmore Hospital in full regalia for a broken back. The x-rays showed no broken bones. Two weeks later I knew that, at least, I had a broken rib, but it was 1.5 years later when I had full spinal x-rays for the osteoporosis specialist that two previously broken vertebrae showed up. At the time of the fall I thought it was very surprising there were "no broken bones" so I wasn't surprised at this news. It had taken about a year of pain before my back was healed. I couldn't believe I could be so stupid.

February. I began to be afraid of February. For a few years I seem to either have a surgery (once for a minor case of cancer) or broken a bone in February. I found I was dreading February. In 1998 I managed to pass February without mishap, then March, only to find myself in April skiing down the east side of Deception Pass in Banff National Park when I caught my skis in rucked up snow, flipped into the air and landed with my skis crossed and jammed my bindings together. As I landed I heard something crack. I had to grit my teeth to force the bindings apart, then get the skis off, stand them crossed in the snow and assess the damage. A friend, who was on the trip with me, was behind and up the slope out of sight. A fellow heading up the pass saw me fall and asked if I needed help. I told him to get my friend. My friend came down and said there was a ski patrol on a snowmobile further up out of sight. He was checking out an avalanche site where people had done a self-rescue. She went and got the patroller, and between them they did the first aid thing and got me onto the snowmobile. At first I fell off as it was at a bad angle, so the patroller said he would get a toboggan. That got me really scared because I didn't want the long wait and I also wasn't going to be stuck in a toboggan going down the side hill of Boulder Pass where it was probable the toboggan would pendulum. So I inched my butt along the snow, with my foot in the air, to the machine and got back up on it and with a little change of direction stayed on and the patroller took me down to Temple Chalet where a vehicle took us to my van and my friend drove it to the Banff hospital with me trussed up in the back. That was the first time in twenty-nine years of skiing that I broke a bone while skiing and had to be rescued. Not a bad average.

When I think of Lizzie Rummel in relation to pain, I remember that she once told me she experienced arthritic pain every day for twenty years, and she lived another ten years with that pain. I, at least, have had gaps in my life when I've been free of pain.

During my sixties my back started bothering me again, but in a different way. By November 2005 I fell twice on hard snow while cross-country skiing and from then on it was pain for part of every day partially controlled with medication. While sitting eating supper prior to having evening guests one night, the pain in my leg from my back was so bad I prayed, "Lord please take this pain away." Two seconds later I received a phone call informing me that one couple would not be coming for the social time as they were helping a neighbour whose son had disappeared two weeks before and had now been found, but the family was in deep crises. When I got off the phone and thought for a minute I realized that I could lie on my mat on the floor and get relief from my leg pain, but when a child creates a pain in your heart there is no relief. I'd rather have the pain in my leg than a pain in my heart.

In March 2008 I had my back surgery. It's a small world though as the neurosurgeon who did the operation told me he used to go to Ribbon Creek Hostel with his son's cub group when I was there. That was thirty plus years ago! Similarly, when I saw an ophthalmologist he told me he also went to the hostel "a lot" when I was there.

It really is a small world.

*T*wo years after my back surgery, just when I thought I had it made, I vacuumed my house and van, something I'd done many times, I ended up in so much back pain I was flat on my back for several months. Many months later I'm still waiting to get it fixed. Hopefully by the time you read this it will be.

Relationships

Kelly

The first dog I bought after a break-in at Ribbon Creek Hostel (See my book *The Valley of Rumors...the Kananaskis*) was Spike, a trained guard dog. I only had him a short time when he started to turn on me. I phoned the man I'd bought him from and explained the problem. "What can I do?" "Nothing" he said. "Bring the dog back and we'll exchange him." He guaranteed his dogs.

When I arrived at the kennels I had to wait a bit. While waiting I chatted with a couple and explained my predicament. The man's eyes lit up because Spike was just the type of dog he wanted.

I got Kelly and the man got Spike and we were both happy.

Kelly was obedience trained, but not guard dog trained. That turned out well because I just needed a diplomatic dog that would protect me. Kelly was exactly that. If he didn't trust someone he would always stand or lie between us. One of the fellows who came to the hostel had been a sheepherder in New Zealand. He gave me a New Zealand sheep dog whistle and taught me how to use it. He also told me that if Kelly didn't trust someone "Don't you trust them." Later I learned how right he was.

Kelly went everywhere with me. Backcountry skiing in the Tonquin Valley for a week, on solo backpack hikes in the summer and all my day hikes and skiing adventures.

I had him for three years and while I was writing my book on Lizzie Rummel in a cabin south of Sundre he got killed. I won't talk about that; it is too painful.

The Shining Presence

Hostelling International had their annual general meeting at the Calgary Zoo theatre one year and invited some of the long time members who used to be active in the Calgary group. Naturally, after running hostels for many years and being a life member, I was invited. It was a special event with goodies and presentations. I believe that was the year Neil Worley, a past president, received special recognition and he was there as well as Ron Hopf and several others with whom I'd hiked and climbed.

When we came out of the meeting it was raining and close to midnight. I still had to drive home to Exshaw over an hour away. By the time I reached the west end of the city the rain was coming down in torrents. Being so late there were not many vehicles on the highway, just a couple of semi-trailer trucks. As I approached the Morley Road my little Nissan truck quit. I coasted to a stop on the side of the road and tried to get it going without any luck.

I got out and opened the back of the canopy, grabbed my emergency sleeping bag and took it into the truck cab. I could lock myself into the cab, but not the canopy. Wrapping the sleeping bag around me I curled up on the seat and went to sleep. I made sure my feet faced the highway and my head faced the ditch. Should the truck be hit I might be maimed, but not killed. Due to the heavy rain there was no one wandering around, so I felt quite safe.

At six o'clock in the morning the rain had stopped and I woke up and tried getting the truck to go. It started feebly and I was able to continue driving west. On the east end of a turnout it quit again and just wouldn't start. Knowing I was only 3 km from a pay phone (I didn't have a cell phone at that time) I started walking west. There were two semi-trailer trucks in the turnout and one had the engine running. As I walked by the one that was running the driver offered me a lift. He obviously had seen me leave my truck.

I climbed into his big truck and noticed a younger man sitting on the bed behind the front seats. As we were driving along I could see out of the corner of my eye a huge shining presence between the younger man and me and that presence was there all the way to Canmore where the trucker dropped me off.

The Date

It was early in the year 1968 and I was living in Calgary. Fraser, one of the guys from the hostel group, asked me to go downhill skiing at Lake Louise. He arranged to pick me up about 6:00 a.m. on Saturday.

I was living in a little basement suite and when Fraser arrived he asked to use my washroom. When I got in the car there was another girl in the front seat. Fraser was my date, but she sat in the middle and talked non-stop all the way to Lake Louise! How do you get to know a guy that way?

Once at Lake Louise the girl disappeared and Fraser and I got on the new Olympic chair lift. It was -20 F. When we got to the top of the lift I didn't get my skis down on the short ramp quick enough and ended up going around the lift turntable. The attendant stopped the lift and I had to take my skis off and drop them and the poles down to the attendant and Fraser. Then I had to lift the front bar, turn around and hang down from the chair and let go, being caught by the two guys.

That over, Fraser and I spent the rest of the day skiing and having an enjoyable time. Later we met up with the girl who came with us and drove back to Calgary. I can't remember where that girl sat in the car this time.

Back home I went into my washroom and discovered I had forgotten I had a drying rack full of lingerie squeezed into this tiny bathroom. Fraser would have almost scraped his nose on them to get in there. I was totally embarrassed.

"He'll never ask me out again after all those faux pas."

Life takes some funny turns though. About eight months later I was in London, England, riding on the Tube when a fellow got on and stood right in front of me reading the Tube map. He looked just like Fraser! I wasn't sure; this was a long way from Lake Louise. When he went over to a seat and sat down his mannerisms made me sure he must be, so I went and touched him on the shoulder. It was Fraser and he was thrilled to see me. That night he took me out to a movie.

So the ski trip wasn't the last date!

Mister Swiss

On my trip to Europe in 1968 the first hostel I stayed in was Houghton Mill Youth Hostel, in England. There was a group of school children in the hostel and one male cyclist from Switzerland. Since I was used to chatting with hostellers I struck up a conversation with the fellow. He asked me how old I was. In Canada you don't ask a woman how old she is, so I said what I always said: "Twenty-five, the same as last year." Unfortunately, I didn't take into account the language barrier. He could speak English, but was not aware of the humor, so he didn't get it. He was twenty-four years old and I was thirty-one. (Remember I look ten years younger than I am.) The next day I saw him off on his bike, but not before he'd invited me to visit his family in Switzerland. I wasn't sure I'd go, but possibly if it worked out.

As it turned out later on I was not far from his home so I contacted him and visited him and his family. The third day I knew him he asked me to marry him. I said no. Obviously he had not told his family this information and his mother, a professional seamstress with a studio in the upstairs of the house, decided she would make me a dress to show I was welcome in the family.

I had been traveling with other young people I'd met in Brussels and I was to meet up with two of the girls and continue to Spain a little later. This meant, when Pat and Ilene arrived, I had to leave before the dress was finished. After our sojourn in Barcelona Pat and I returned. She was going to Wales for Christmas and I was going to my friends the van Heijsts in Holland. En route we would stop at Mister Swiss' home for the dress. The only problem was I got sick in Spain and by the time we got to Geneva I ended up in hospital for nine days.

As soon as I got out of hospital Pat and I headed to Mister Swiss' home. Not long after getting there I got sick again. This created a crisis. Mister Swiss spoke English, the family spoke German and his mother spoke a little French as well. Fortunately Pat spoke fluent French. I knew a couple of dozen words in French and no German.

There was a big confrontation between Pat and the mother about the mother getting an English speaking doctor for me so I would stay there, but Pat and I both realized I had to get out of this stressful situation and get to my friends in Holland.

Finally, in spite of the mother's protestations, Pat and I left and I ended up in Holland with my friends. Two days later I was back in hospital, this time in Rotterdam for eight days. I spent Christmas in hospital where I was treated royally—after all I was a Canadian. Furthermore, I could do no wrong as I was born in the same hospital in Ottawa as the Dutch princesses had been during World War II. Not at the same time, of course.

Six months after returning home, the saga continues. Mister Swiss arrived in Calgary with another dress in his hand, slept on the living room floor of the house my roommate and I shared for six weeks, and then rented an apartment around the corner. I still wasn't in the marrying mood.

Sometime later two female friends and I went downhill skiing at Sunshine where I met a girl who had recently been jilted by a Swiss guy. I introduced her to the hostel group and thus to Mister Swiss. The rest is history.

Lizzie Rummel

The hostel group in Calgary ran backpack hiking trips every weekend in the summer when I joined in 1967. I was living in Calgary in the late 1960s when the August long weekend trip to Mount Assiniboine came up. At that time I was a regular hiker with the group, so naturally I went along.

Those were the days when you drove down the west side road by Spray Lakes Reservoir to Bryant Creek. A death defying feat considering the state of the road. After taking our lives in our hands on the road, we hiked into Mount Assiniboine from the Bryant Creek junction.

While at Mount Assiniboine Tom Wilcock, one of the fellows on the trip, said, "Let's go to Lizzie's for tea." Because I didn't have any money to pay for tea I wouldn't go, even though Tom insisted and said you didn't have to pay for tea at Lizzie's.

The next time Lizzie came to my attention was 1970 when I was running Eisenhower Hostel. One of my hostellers had been in the Whyte Museum Archives and met Lizzie who was doing volunteer work there. She told Lizzie about me at the hostel and Lizzie said, "You tell her to come and see me." I felt obliged to do so and thus met her. After that I would regularly have a visit and tea at her house in Canmore and help her out and she occasionally visited me, along with Muriel Gratz, at the hostel.

When the opportunity arose for me to do some relief cooking at Bugaboo Lodge in January 1972, Hans Gmoser's heli-ski place, Lizzie came and looked after the hostel for me. She thoroughly spoiled the regular hostellers, doing their dishes and cleaning up after them. I had to retrain them when I got back! She said it gave her something to do.

In 1971 and 1972 I got a job as cook at Skoki Lodge in July and August. Lizzie was thrilled. She thought I was following in her footsteps of running Skoki Lodge. However, that wasn't the plan for me, my life took a different turn.

In those days I never dreamt she would become an integral part of my life. Not only when she was alive, but also long after she died.

In January 1980, while working as a cook at the University of Calgary's Kananaskis field station I had a strong feeling that I was to save my money. After running hostels for 8.5 years and living on a dime that wasn't difficult. By June I realized I didn't want to spend the rest of my working life cooking 12 hours a day, so in July I quit and moved to a little cabin 16 km south of Sundre, Alberta, with the plan of spending a year weaving and writing to see if I could earn my living that way. I had been weaving for profit for some time.

In October 1980 when Lizzie was dying I was asked to look after the Alpine Club of Canada's clubhouse on the slopes of Grotto Mountain just outside of Canmore for a week. While there I visited Lizzie in the Canmore hospital.

A few days after she died I was hiking up Grotto Creek and met Lloyd (Kiwi) and Fran Gallagher and their little sons. We talked about Lizzie and Kiwi said to me "You are the one to write Lizzie's story." Everyone who knew Lizzie wanted her story written. I was in the right place, so I spent the next year doing just that.

During my friendship with Lizzie I had became friends with her sister Jane Fisher. Jane had moved into the senior's home in Canmore from the ranch near Millarville. Her husband of 47 years had left her for his mistress and she was devastated and embarrassed. She couldn't face her ranching friends. When I started writing Lizzie's biography Jane was a tremendous help. She filled me in on their life in Europe and the early days on their ranch. When my book came out it was sold in the Millarville area, among other places, and suddenly Jane was a star! She, Lizzie, and their family were in the book. She regained face. Her sons had been pressuring her to move to the seniors' home in Black Diamond to be closer to them, but she wouldn't go, however, once she realized she had become a celebrity in the ranching community through my book about Lizzie, she did go to Black Diamond to live in the extended care unit.

As a sequel to that, her husband Joe had a spiritual catharsis and left his mistress, apologized to ~~Lizzie~~ Jane for his years of infidelity, and moved into the seniors' lodge next door to the extended care unit. While they didn't have much in common Jane said, he religiously came to visit her once a week and spent the day sitting in her room with her. His penitence was real. As an aside, Joe Fisher had been a bronc rider in the first Calgary Stampede in 1912.

Some years after Lizzie died and my biography of her was on the market I was working at the Barrier Lake Visitor Information Centre in Kananaskis Country. One day two ladies approached me at the counter and were talking about Lizzie. It turned out that one of them had read my book about Lizzie. That lady told me she had been in hospital for depression and someone gave her my book. She read the book, put it down and walked out of the hospital cured! She realized that her life wasn't as hard as Lizzie's.

Another time, a lady came into the information centre and told me she had deliberately visited every place in the mountains mentioned in my book.

The year after *Ruthie's Little Hiking Group* came into being I took nineteen of my group into Mount Assiniboine for four days of hiking. We stayed in the Naiset Cabins. Our first day's hike took us past what had been Lizzie's cabin when she was in the mountain lodge business. I sat everyone on the benches on the porch of the cabin and told them about Lizzie. That evening we formed a circle in front of one of our cabins and I told them more. It was surprising to me at how emotional I became from re-visiting where she spent so many years. It was like she was right there with me. I loved Lizzie and over the time I knew her and spent researching and writing her biography I came to admire her very much. She was an amazing inspiration to me as well as to many other people.

Lizzie's Cabin at Mount Assiniboine, 2006. Photo: Jean McLennan.

Chapter 7

Kananaskis Country Information Centres

Ruthie at the Barrier Lake Visitor Information Centre her last day working there, April 30, 2000.

A New Career

*M*y book about Lizzie Rummel was almost finished in August of 1981 and my money was as well, so I started looking for a job. After spending a year living in a small cabin in the rolling farmland south of Sundre, Alberta, I knew I had to go back to live in the mountains. I wasn't having much luck with the job-hunting though.

While complaining to Barb Long (Snyder) about this, she told me that maybe I was supposed to finish the book.

"Oh."

So I knuckled down and finished the book and promptly got a job I had previously applied for at the Barrier Lake Travel Information Centre in Kananaskis Country. The centre was operated by Travel Alberta, part of the provincial government. At the start of my second summer Barb Spencer, our Edmonton boss, asked me go to Cold Lake and supervise an information centre. This was a very quiet centre—fifteen people in one day was a busy day! However, the political maneuvering of a certain lady was not quiet. I ended up being manipulated into attending a dinner that was composed of the Alberta and Saskatchewan tourism ministers. Just as I was congratulating myself on being a successful wallflower the best looking young man in the room came and spoke to me. I think his job was to entertain wallflowers. Later I got questions directed at me that made me wish I'd melted into that wall.

The next four summers I supervised the Canmore Travel Information Centre and worked at the Barrier Lake Centre in the winter. The last two of those years was supervising the Canmore centre and the Barrier Lake Centre year round. Eventually Travel Alberta transferred its two information centres in Kananaskis Country (Barrier Lake and Elbow Valley) to the Parks department and my job went with the transfer.

During my nineteen years working in the information centres I ended up supervising, not only the Barrier Lake Centre, but also the Elbow Valley Visitor Centre, the Sheep River Information Centre (weekends in summer), Bow Valley Provincial Park centre (weekends in summer), Kananaskis Village Post Office and Information Centre and Peter Lougheed Provincial Park Information Centre.

Some of this time was during the government cut backs to pay off the provincial debt so there were a lot of changes taking place. Fortunately, I thrive on change. Just when I would be getting bored something would change. I had thirteen bosses in nineteen years, although two of them were only for two weeks each. Joel Christensen was my boss three times, so I called him my recycled boss.

It was particularly enjoyable working with my various staff. I became very fond of them all. I met the mothers of several of the young people and they always thought of me as a surrogate mother to their kids. I thus had dozens of children and they taught me a lot, like most children do.

After I'd been hiking for thirty plus years Tamara Kraynick, one of my young staff members, taught me how to tie my hiking boots! You're never too old to learn.

One busy day when I was working in the Barrier Lake Centre a young man came in, wove his way around the people waiting to be served, leaned across the information counter beside the person I was helping, and said to me: "When are they going to cut off your leg and count the rings to see how long you've been here?"

Another day one of my regular visitors came into the Barrier Lake Centre on a quiet afternoon. We chatted about cross-country skiing and gradually he opened up and talked about his wife who had Multiple Sclerosis and was in a wheelchair, and all the problems that he encountered with care givers, and the thousands of dollars he had spent on her teeth. By the time he left I was overwhelmed with the knowledge that we just don't know what kind of burdens people are carrying around when they walk into the information centre door. It made me become even more helpful and gracious to our visitors. I wanted to be a bright light in people's lives to help ease their burdens.

One day a gentleman of about sixty years was asking me about doing the Kananaskis circle drive—south on Highway 40 and north on the Smith-Dorrien/Spray Trail road to Canmore. He was very concerned about the gravel road and hesitant to drive it. Finally, without thinking, I said, "Oh go for it, you're only young once." His eyes lit up and his brain came into gear and off he went.

At one time I required another staff person in the Elbow Valley Visitor Centre south of Bragg Creek Village. I had two applicants for the job. Brenda Dennis and Jean McLennan, the latter a lady with white hair. Brenda got the job as she had more experience and knowledge of Kananaskis and the Elbow Valley in particular. However, two weeks after she started she was offered a job that was what she was trained for in Cochrane, where she lived, so she left the visitor centre.

At the time I was hiring when Jean found out she didn't get the job she had called and asked if it was because of her age. I said no, of course not, and laughed to myself because she is a year younger than me. Initially she had been interested in her daughters working in the information centre, but they suggested she apply.

After Brenda quit I offered the job to Jean and she accepted. She worked in the information centres for about ten years and was an excellent information officer and is still a great friend.

When Jean started she said she would not hike alone, which was necessary to learn about the trails. I didn't have the budget for two staff to do familiarization hikes together and still have someone in the information centre. With my consent she would invite her husband or a friend to accompany her. As time went by and she felt more comfortable on the trails, she started doing some hiking alone. She eventually did a lot of solo hiking. So much so that one time on her two days off she hiked the Little Elbow/Big Elbow 43 km loop and stayed overnight in the Fish and Wildlife cabin at Sheep Lakes, the apex of the loop.

You've come a long way baby!

Missing Link Trail

Willa Stomp started working for me at the Elbow Valley Visitor Information Centre when she was sixteen years old. She worked her way through high school, university, and then a year full time at Kananaskis Village Centre while she tried to get on with the R.C.M.P. She subsequently achieved her goal and I was thrilled to attend her R.C.M.P. graduation in Regina and later her wedding at Whistler, B.C.

This story is about her trail familiarization day when she hiked Missing Link Trail

Willa Stomp and Striker at the Sheep River Visitor Information Centre, 1993.

The EVIC chicks and gosling Don, a.k.a. Jean McLennan, Don Den Hoed and Monique Keiran. At the Elbow Valley Visitor Information Centre, 1992.

in the Sheep River district of Kananaskis. She took along her large dog Striker. Her hike was going very well until she came to a creek crossing that was flowing rather fast and dirty so she couldn't see the bottom. However, it looked simple enough to jump across even though she would land in a bit of water on the other side. So she jumped. Unfortunately, the creek was much deeper than it appeared and she landed in deep water up to her neck! Although totally soaked she managed to get out on the other side of the creek. Striker had an even bigger problem. He made a flying leap and landed completely submerged in the creek, rose to the surface and sunk again, eventually also getting out. Willa, of course, wasn't going to return the same way, so hiked to the Gorge Creek Trail road knowing that the second shift ranger would be coming down that road very shortly. She hitched a ride with him and went home to dry out.

The Funniest Guy

Visitors to information centres don't see some of the funny things that happen to the staff. Don Den Hoed was also sixteen years old when he started working for me at the Elbow Valley Visitor Centre. He has a great sense of humor. Since I had my office at the Barrier Lake Centre the staff in the other centres faxed over a good morning message to me so I knew their centre was open and all was well. We had short forms for the names of the various centres. BVIC was Barrier Lake Visitor Centre, EVIC was the Elbow Valley Visitor Centre, and so forth. Don had the funniest good morning messages.

Good Morning BVIC
Camp is fun
Send more socks
Your son
—EVIC

Good a.m. Barrier
Thought for the day
"The closest we ever come to perfection is when we write our resumes."
—EVIC

Seasons Greetings
From the Supreme Ruler of Kananaskis
Guten tag, Barrier!
Jeanie and I have decided to turn the Visitor centre into an impenetrable fortress and declare Kananaskis Country to be an independent state. You may hereafter refer to us as:
Supreme Ruler - Don Den Hoed
Dictator for Life - Jean McLennan
And that Stupid Squirrel Bob
Our succession from Canada is complete.
Vive la Kananaskis!!

Don couldn't spell secession and the visitor centre had frequent visits from a flying squirrel.

Don left my employ to be a park interpreter in Kananaskis and has risen to great heights and is still working for Kananaskis Country many years later, now as Communications and Outreach Coordinator and goes by his full name Don Carruthers Den Hoed.

No Socks!

One day when Jamie Carpenter started first shift at the Barrier Lake Centre he arrived wearing sandals, but forgot his socks. He called me at home to see if I could loan him some socks. I managed to find a pair of stretchy socks for his size twelve feet. Mine are a size six. While he put them on I took his picture for *The Album*.

The Album

Ten years before I retired I started taking photos each summer of all my staff. I would put them in a big album that I kept on my desk. At first when I wanted to take their picture they were very shy. "Aw shucks" was the usual attitude. Then when they realized their photo was going in *The Album* they would pose. After a few years when a new person started working for us the long-term staff would show them the album and proudly tell them their picture would be in there too. By the time I retired I had two big albums of photos of "my girls and guys." They are a wonderful memento of this memorable time in my life.

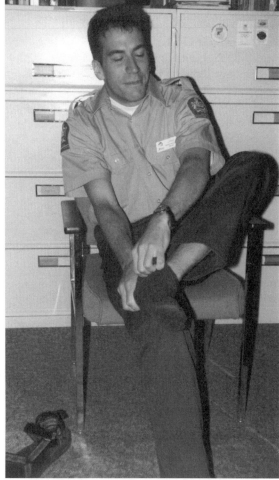

Jamie Carpenter at Barrier Lake
Visitor Information Centre, 1997.

A Kananaskis Country Christmas
It was the day before Christmas
When all through the information centres
All creatures were stirring
Yes even the fires
The brochures were all stacked
By the counters with care
In hopes that visitors
Soon would be there.
The staff were all ready a rarin' to talk, to tell all the visitors just where to go.
The ski trails were all groomed by the trail crew with care, in hopes the visitors soon
would be there.
The visitors were all geared up
And rarin' to go
With their ski maps in hand
Their hats on their heads
They tore off on their skis
In a mad snowy rush
To view the great scenery, to get some good exercise, to ward off heart surgery, they
skied into the snow in the hope they'd have fun with good old Saint Nicholas

By the end of the Christmas week the staff were all tired, but happy they'd helped all
the visitors who came.

On Ruthie, on Gwen, on Mavis and Paula
On Willa and Jean
And all those fun friends.
Three cheers To the Kananaskis Country staff who worked Christmas week.
Unstinting their labours, unfailing their enthusiasm. Yeah, Yeah, Yeah You good guys
we love you all.
Have a Merry Christmas one and all

Compassionate Hearts

May 1st, 1999 found me in the Barrier Lake Visitor Information Center in Kananaskis Country. When I answered the phone it was a call from Doris Popowich of the Make a Wish Foundation in Edmonton. She told me of a little boy who had leukemia and had only three weeks to live. Most kids want to go to Disneyland, but this little boy wanted to camp in a motor home in Kananaskis Country. She had arranged for a motor home to be taken to the Mount Kidd R.V. Park and the family would go from Edmonton to Jasper, down to Banff and then to Kananaskis Country. Doris wondered if the rangers, or someone in Kananaskis, could do something extra special for this little boy. I promised to help.

I called the Kananaskis Country interpreters, but they were going to be in the middle of a retreat and couldn't see how they could swing something. I tried calling a ranger; any ranger would do, but couldn't get hold of anyone. I wasn't about to give up, so I took my notes home and tried Glenn Naylor at home as he was the head ranger of that area of Kananaskis Country. I had to leave a message on his answering machine, but at 9:30 that night he called me back. He had spent the whole day at the Canmore Trade Fair and had just got home. When I told him the story, he immediately rose to the occasion and said, yes, he would get some rangers to do something. He didn't know what, but the following Monday there was a big ranger meeting and he would bring up the subject and see what would happen.

I called Doris and told her yes, something would happen, but it would be a big secret until the last minute. Doris said the boy had a blood transfusion just before the family left for Jasper and arrangements had been made to get another one in Calgary if necessary—so he would feel well enough to enjoy the trip.

The big ranger meeting happened on the Monday and Glenn brought up the subject of the little boy with leukemia and every ranger in the room who had children raised their hands and said they would help.

The boy and his family were coming on the Wednesday, so there wasn't much time, however, the rangers outdid themselves. First of all Glenn had told everyone, "No pity. Treat him like any kid." And they did.

When the crew of rangers arrived at the Mount Kidd R.V. Park, Glenn met a member of the family at the Campers' Center and they went over to the campsite and met the boy and talked with him a bit. Then they gave him a certificate saying he was an Honorary Park Ranger for the day. Glenn gave him a copy of his photograph book of Kananaskis Country and I had asked The Friends of Kananaskis to donate a Mountain Alphabet book, which he also gave to the boy. Glenn then drove the boy and his sister over to the campground parking lot.

When they arrived there were three fire trucks, an Emergency Response Vehicle, two horses and ranger Nikki Lepage with her search and rescue dog. They also had a bear trap, the Jaws-of-Life and an old car.

The boy was given a choice of which fire truck he wanted a ride in, as well as a tour of the Emergency Services Response vehicle. They also had some telemetry equipment for tracking bears that they demonstrated for him. They locked him in the bear trap and showed him how it worked with bears. Using the Jaws-of-Life they tore apart the old car and gave both children a piece of the car. Ranger Mike O'Reilly gave the two of them a horseback ride, and then Glenn hid with the boy and Nikki Lepage did a search for them with her search and rescue dog.

Throughout all this activity there were photographs and videos taken. Before it was all over Glenn gave the boy his own personal ranger hat and a Mountain Rescue hat and pin as well.

The following rangers were involved: Glenn Naylor, Nikki Lepage, Mike O'Reilly, Jay Honeyman, Dave Humphrey, Dave Hoff and five or six fire fighters from the Kananaskis Emergency Services fire hall.

It was a whole morning and by the time it was all over there was a happy boy, although very tired. The rangers of Kananaskis Country showed their true compassion and their willingness to drop everything for a little boy with three weeks to live.

A Cooler of Beer

One afternoon a lady came into the Barrier Lake Visitor Centre and complained to me that she had met two young guys on the Galatea Creek Trail who were back-packing into Lillian Lake and were carrying a big cooler full of beer between them. They also had their big packs on their backs.

"They shouldn't be allowed to do that," she said. "It's not right," etc., etc. Finally I leaned over the counter and whispered to her, "Don't worry. That cooler will be so heavy they will never do it again."

"Oh," she said. "I never thought of that."

Retirement

*A*fter six years of over two dozen health problems I was getting tired and I was 63 years old. One morning I woke up and before lifting my head off the pillow I looked at Mount McGillivray, which was perfectly framed in the bedroom window, and my first thought was "I am going to retire." One month later I did.

After my last day of work, May 2, 2000, (Official retirement June 24, 2000) I took a couple of trips and then returned for my retirement party.

Retirement Party Speech Notes

Alberta Government Alberta Environment/Natural Resources Service
Kananaskis Country Information Centres

I'm not just retiring from nineteen years in my government job, but from a forty-six year working career.

Looking back:

My first job was in 1954 as a stenographer with the United Kingdom Air Liaison Staff in Ottawa with a salary of 125 dollars a month. I took shorthand and typed on a Royal standard typewriter and could type 83 words a minute. In those days we used carbon paper and Gestetners for duplicating.

In 1955 I went to Central Baptist Seminary in Toronto for three years and worked part time in offices.

After seminary I worked as a legal and executive secretary in Toronto and Calgary. I used IBM typewriters: Electric, Executive Electric, Selectric and used carbon paper for copies.

I came to the mountains in 1970 to run a hostel for the summer, and I'm still in the mountains. I ran hostels for 8.5 years (Spray River, Eisenhower, now called Castle Mountain, and Ribbon Creek, now called Kananaskis Wilderness Hostel). I had to work part time to supplement my income, so I cleaned cabins at Johnston Canyon and Castle Mountain, and I worked for the University of Calgary's Kananaskis field station where I wrote my first history book. Dr. Gordon Hodgson was my supervisor. I also wrote the first trail guide to the Kananaskis Valley.

In 1980 I took a year off working at a job to weave and write and wrote my book about Lizzie Rummel.

I finished Lizzie, ran out of money and got my job at the Barrier Lake Visitor Centre in October 1981.

I started out in the Department of Tourism that lasted for 6.5 years.

In 1988 I was transferred to Parks and all the subsequent changes that have taken place since then.

I was 44 years old when I started this job, an age when lots of people were moaning that they were too old to get a job. It never crossed my mind that I wouldn't get a job. It has been the best job I've ever had with good money and many challenges. (A big jump from 125 dollars a month) I had great people to work with. I started supervising in the summer of 1983 at Grand Centre/Cold Lake, and supervised Canmore Travel Information Centre four summers and two winters and one of those winters I did Barrier Lake and Canmore. I supervised Elbow Valley Visitor Centre (formerly Gooseberry) for eleven years and Sheep River Visitor Centre on weekends for three or four years, Kananaskis Village for four years, Bow Valley Provincial Park summers, Peter Lougheed Park Visitor Centre for two years and Barrier Lake, more or less for twelve years.

Lots of people worked for me. Initially, when we were Travel Alberta, the head office in Edmonton did the hiring, then Joel Christensen did the hiring when I first became Parks and eventually I did my own hiring. I only fired one person and she thanked me for firing her and I'm proud of her. She changed her life around and got it together.

The funniest employee I've ever had is Don Den Hoed—the Supreme Ruler of Kananaskis! The most charming employee is Jamie Carpenter. And if you're going to break an ankle on Deception Pass I recommend having Carol

Ruthie and Wayne Grams at Barrier Lake Visitor Information Centre, 2000.

Mehling along as she thrives on patching people up.

People like Jean McLennan, Willa Stomp, Brenda Evans, Sue Clarke, Tamara Kraynick and BK Thompson who's now my house sitter—there are a score of people I could mention. But, overall, the best employee I've ever had is Wayne Grams—he has such a wide variety of talents and understanding that he is a gem. But everyone has been special in different ways. Some I've worried about a lot, some have never caused me a moment's worry. I'm still friends with many of my former employees who are terrific people.

There's a verse in the Bible that says *More are the children of the desolate woman than of her who has a husband.* I don't feel desolate, but I've sure had lots of children if you want to call them that.

There has been lots of variety and lots of changes. I went from using my own standard, portable typewriter to government electric typewriters, to a word processor, to several different computers, a teleprinter during Tourism days, faxes, Internet, and e-mail.

My sixteen years working in offices prepared me for the administrative end of the information centres job. My hostel managership prepared me for dealing with people. While I made some mistakes I also learned a lot. In my 46 years of working I've never collected a penny of unemployment insurance, nor a penny of Social Assistance. I've been fired from three jobs—two house-keeping jobs that I tried when in Seminary and the last job I had in Calgary, a secretarial one. The last firing capitulated me into the mountains and changed my life forever! I've always found a job when I wanted one.

If you had told me when I was 17 years old that I was going to work for 46 years I'd have been depressed for days. Fortunately we don't see the future and we can take one day at a time.

You never know where you can go in life until you get in there and work and be willing to do all kinds of things. I've been a cook: at Skoki Lodge, Bugaboo Lodge (relief cook), Assiniboine Lodge (ACC), and at the U. of C. Kananaskis field station. I've been willing to scrub floors—and I've done that. I've helicopter skied for free at the Bugaboos because of that job (32,000 feet). I've seen all kinds of wonderful places and met many wonderful people—cow-boys, research scientists, lots of very talented people. I've made friends with some of our information centre visitors. I've written four books and have another in the works I'm going to get serious about.

My government job has been the best. I've worked with many wonderful people, both as employees, as peers, and in work relationships. Everyone has really enhanced my life and made it richer and rewarding. Thank you.

Just before I finished work I learned the meaning of the word *wrench*, but I did my wrenching away from the job before I left, so that once I left I was too busy to miss it. I've been enjoying myself so much that I haven't had time to go to the information centers and ask obscure questions, but I will, just you wait. I'm enjoying not having to answer the bear question and I'll enjoy not having to answer the avalanche question next winter. I'm enjoying not having all that responsibility too. I enjoyed it at the time, but I've been getting tired.

It was time to retire. All you who thought I was married to the job made a mistake; it's the Kananaskis I'm married to!

Thank you all for being here and celebrating with me my 19 years with the government and my 46 years in the work force.

To say my career in the information centres enhanced my life and introduced me to marvellous people would be a grand understatement. There were lots of hard times, and times when I was stretched to my limit, but there were many good times, and I wouldn't have missed the adventure for the world. I learned a tremendous amount about people, about administration, about new technology, and worked with many wonderful people. It was my most rewarding job in my career and the best paying job I'd ever had, and I'm enjoying the pension!

The Other Side of the Counter

Published in The Friends of Kananaskis Country newsletter The Spirit of Kananaskis. Summer 2000

Hands clapping, feet stomping and great shouts of approval reverberate throughout the Elkwood Amphitheatre in Peter Lougheed Provincial Park. These are the sounds of another popular night of interpretative programming

Barrier Lake Visitor Information Centre.

in Kananaskis Country. The amphitheatres fill to overflowing with enthusiastic campers and visitors on many nights throughout the summer as the interpretative staff tell a story about the natural environment through drama, song and dance. This summer I was right in there along with several hundred other people, clapping my hands and stomping my feet and being enthusiastic. I've attended more amphitheatre programs this summer than ever before and have developed a better understanding of how campers relate to the programs. One of the joys of retirement is that I don't have to worry about getting up at six-thirty in the morning and being bright and cheerful at the information centre counter. Now I can go camping and stay up late at night and sleep in.

It has been rewarding to meet up with information centre visitors at the amphitheatre programs and on the trails and to hear their enthusiastic responses to the programs and Kananaskis in general. I've been impressed with the camper participants' enthusiasm and knowledge of how amphitheatre programs work. They all seem to know that they are expected to participate in some way in each program; maybe by holding up signs, or actually being on the stage and doing things, or just hooting and hollering their answers and enthusiasm. This enthusiasm is infectious and I find myself carried right along. It's great to be a kid again, even if it is my second childhood!

In the past my camping in Kananaskis Country has always been wonderful, but it has been coupled with major hikes or scrambles, so I haven't taken the time to watch the campers and be part of the family scenes around a campfire. This first summer of retirement saw me camping in Elkwood Campground at the end of July with retired friends and their children and grandchildren. Watching kids cycling around the campground and the bike trail, and parents rollerblading and me hiking Marl Lake Trail at a leisurely pace was a lot of fun. Now I don't have to rush to get out on the big hikes all the time and can enjoy the small hikes as well. Previously I would do three or four small hikes in a day so I was aware of conditions first hand, but now I can do them one at a time.

This summer I have been able to observe the extent to which campers utilize the campgrounds. It is not just an overnight stop to them. While some people just sit around their campsite and enjoy the environment, others get very active and disappear onto a trail for the day, while others do the cycling and rollerblading and back for lunch scenario, or go to Boulton Creek Trading Post for ice cream and other goodies. I sensed a very family atmosphere throughout the campgrounds. Kananaskis has definitely become a very special place to a lot of people.

While I've noticed things in the campgrounds, it has also been interesting to arrive at the information centres and be on the other side of the counter. Nineteen years on the staff side of the counter makes for a new adjustment when on the visitors' side. It sure feels different and makes for quite a change. I know how tired the staff are in late August and yet how helpful they still can be, but now I know when to cruise around the Friends of Kananaskis Shop while the centre is busy (I'm still buying presents and cards in this great place) and I can understand why visitors look at the displays while they wait to be helped by the staff. I'm already missing our visitors and that wonderful contact, in spite of the fact that I'm enjoying retirement.

As well, my marriage to the Kananaskis is still intact. I can still be found in many places in Kananaskis Country. For instance, in early July I just had to go up to Highwood Pass, just to see it and be in that marvellous meadow. At the time I was recovering from a knee injury and couldn't hike, but I could look at the scenery. When four or five conservation officers showed up in the parking lot I knew from my experience in the information centres that Bear No. 24 or one of her cubs must be around. Sure enough, when I asked Jay Honeyman what was happening he said it was one of Bear No. 24's older cubs up on the slope near the Ptarmigan Cirque Trail. Sure enough, we could see the bear from the parking lot. He was busy eating and not at all interested in humans. So I got the bear report before the information centres did! Now that's a change.

It's taking awhile to get used to not feeling a need to go out to hike trails just so that I know firsthand what the conditions are like. However, it is nice to still be able to talk to the people I worked with in the information centres and the head office in Canmore. It's been a lot of fun going to the amphitheatre programs and camping and hiking as a visitor and observing everyone having a good time.

Keep up the good work Kananaskis gang—I'll see you in the stands and on the trails.

Chapter 9
Wildlife & Other Stories

Kelly and Ruthie on Skogan Pass, 1977. Photo: Flo Smith.

Lots of Stories to Share

Wildlife in Victoria

Exert from an email from Peggy Magee dated May 4, 2007.

"A few days ago, a mama duck marched into the centre of Oak Bay Avenue with eleven new hatchlings. The owner of the bookstore, where Diana works, sent one of the clerks out to escort the family across Oak Bay Avenue and to follow them all the way to the creek, about four blocks, and to stop traffic, no matter what. Then she sent Diana out the next day to the creek to count and all eleven were there!"

Pasque Mountain Bears

Bill and Lucille Pulliam and I started out on a hike to Pasque Mountain in the Highwood region of Kananaskis Country one fine summer day. We followed an old logging road, crossed a creek on a bridge and were just going up a rise walking three abreast when we startled a sow grizzly with two big cubs. The bears took off in one direction and we in the direction we had come. At one point I turned around because I wanted to see the sun glimmering on the bear's rippling fur as she ran, however, she turned around to watch us too, so we just kept going. We changed our destination to Plateau Mountain, but considered it a rare privilege to see the beautiful bears.

Missed Encounter

Published in the Alpine Club of Canada, Rocky Mountain Section newsletter The Blizzard July 2004

An hour and a half to spare while attending a convention in Banff led me to the Fenland Trail on June 4th for a little exercise. The low bushes were not in leaf yet, but the trail was dry, and meandering along at a casual pace was very pleasant. I stepped off the trail a couple of times to let three cyclists pass. I was almost back to the bridge to the parking lot when I saw a brown animal run across the trail ahead of me. He was moving fairly fast so at first I couldn't tell what it was. I watched to see where it was going and to my surprise it was a grizzly bear, maybe two or three years old. I didn't feel like going back the way I came, as I was so close to the trailhead, and I didn't know what direction the bear was going. Yikes, he was coming in my direction! What do I do?

He was moving along in the woods to the right of the trail. I hesitated and then went into the woods to the left of the trail. It wasn't thick leafy woods, so I hid behind two trees that were growing close together. Since the bear hadn't seen me I kept quiet, as I didn't want to let him know I was there and give him the idea of coming to see me. He was moving parallel to the trail and seemed intent on sniffing or eating as he walked. Since I am kind of slim and the tree was kind of thick, I just moved around the tree as he moved and he walked by about fifty feet away. I didn't do any of the yelling and screaming we are always told to do to let the bears know you are there—I didn't want him to know I was there! I just kept peeking around the tree to see where he was and moving around the tree as he moved along. He never once looked towards me from what I could tell. Once I couldn't see him anymore I high-tailed it to the parking lot.

I must admit my heart did go pitter-pat a few times and I did utter a quick prayer and you can bet I did heave a sigh of relief when I got to my van.

The moral of this story is: there is a time and place in life to keep your mouth shut.

Momma and Baby Bear

The Deer Ridge and Eagle Hill trails combination was our destination on another sunny day when I was leading a group of nine people. We had just passed the pond at the beginning of Deer Ridge Trail and were heading up into the woods when I saw something black that I couldn't quite make out. As I got closer I saw a little black thing moving. It was a mother black bear playing with her cub. She was batting the cub and it would roll and run back to her for more and she would bat it again. I immediately turned my group around and we took a different route to Eagle Hill. Momma bear never knew we were there as her back was toward us. Once more it was a case of there is a time and place in life when it pays to keep your mouth shut.

The Cooking Pots

Four of us, Arnold and Janet Hartford from Ontario, and Donna Iddings and I from the Rockies, flew to Robson Pass in Mount Robson Provincial Park, British Columbia, in 2005. The last time I'd been there was in 1967 with Leslie Moynihan, Charlie Locke, and other Calgary hostellers, so this was a real treat. We were no longer spring chickens, hence the flight.

Arnold and Janet stayed one night and hiked out in two days, Donna and I stayed three nights and hiked out in one day. While there we hiked into Mumm Basin and to Hargreaves Lake with their constantly amazing views of Mount Robson and its tumbling glaciers flowing into Berg Lake. Our really spectacular day was a ten-hour hike to Snowbird Pass. Hiking along the knife-edged moraine with the Robson Glacier far below just took our breath away, and the alpine meadows below the pass were prolific with flowers.

We had good weather except for the last evening when it rained a bit. Because of this Donna and I went to the cook cabin to make dinner. Previously we'd been cooking at our campsite. After dinner when we left the cook cabin we put our food bags in the metal storage bin. I was carrying my 30-year old cooking pots in the nice little waterproof drawstring bag I had made. Donna asked if I was going to put the pots in the storage bin. I said, "No, I don't want them to get stolen." As we walked back to the campsite Donna, walking in front of me, was chuckling away. Finally I asked her what she was laughing about. She said, "You think those young people with their high tech gear are going to steal your old cooking pots!"

Reliable Directions

Email from: Valli Schuering
Date: April 24, 2008 8:00:32 AM MDT

Dear Ruthie,

We were happy to hear that you are out for hikes and doing great. This is wonderful news for the summer hiking season in which we hope to be part of your "clan".

I have to tell you a story that will probably make you smile. Being directionally challenged I wanted a GPS for the car for my birthday last year and have found "the thing" very helpful especially when on our trips we rent cars in strange cities. I just follow "the thing" blindly. Now here is the hitch: it only has a female voice. And you know how men have selective hearing when it comes to female voices!!! Mike had terrible trouble with "her" and kept questioning "her" all the time. Well, yesterday, as we drove along she gave him instructions (which man will take this well?) he lost it and I asked him to just listen to "her" and go. Well, of course, "she" was right! So I decided to name "her". I named her *Ruthie* as Ruthie always knows where she is and always finds her way around anywhere. So now, if Mike gets upset with her and questions her he has to apologize to *Ruthie*!!! After every trip it will be "thank you Ruthie."

We are off to let *Ruthie* guide us into Melbourne where we will visit fellow boater friends.

All the best and continued good recovery.

Love, Valli

Dogs on the Trail

Published in Dogs in Canada magazine—c. 1980

The Canadian Rockies is a wild and beautiful place where peace and serenity can be found, especially for the hiker and cross-country skier. It is also a good place for a dog and a girl to roam together. My German shepherd dog, Kelly, and I roam the mountains, both summer and winter.

While many hikers say that dogs should not be on the trails, a properly trained dog is often kinder to the mountains than some people. Large or medium-sized dogs are better suited to mountain travel than small, talkative dogs, which are sometimes a menace when meeting bears. I recall one time when I passed close to a lynx crouched in the bushes. Kelly immediately charged the lynx and chased it far away, one indication that larger dogs protect their masters against wild animals.

As Kelly and I hike together in the mountains he is a reassuring comfort when crossing streams. Our first creek fording occurred when we had only been together about one week. The stream was thigh deep and moving very fast. I checked carefully for the easiest spot to cross, sat down on the edge of the water, took off my hiking boots and put on wading runners. In the meantime, Kelly ran up and down the edge of the creek, in and out of the water, having a good time. As I hoisted my pack on my back, boots strapped on top, and started across the stream Kelly followed. He soon realized he would have to swim in the deepest spot and to this day he does not like swimming, so back to the shore he ran and tried to find a shallow crossing. Discovering I had taken the best route he did follow, swimming in the deep spot and reaching me as I removed my runners. On our return journey, never blinking an eye, he stepped into the water beside me and stayed there all the way to the opposite shore. From that time on he always walked beside me when fording streams. I grew confident he would rescue me should I be swept downstream.

Our day hikes progressed naturally into overnight hiking trips and eventually overnight skiing trips. On our overnight trips Kelly carries his own pack, a set of bright red saddlebags, with his food and occasionally an item or two of mine. He waits patiently while I buckle on his pack before jumping for joy because we are going on a trip. Sleeping in a tent, high in the mountains has become a real joy to Kelly. While I putter around the campsite he lays quietly nearby, occasionally deciding to lie in the tent away from the mosquitoes. When this happens he butts the screening on the tent doorway with his nose until I let him inside. Once inside the tent he lays his nose on his paws and contemplates me with his big brown eyes.

On one of our trips we skied for six days in the Tonquin Valley in Jasper National Park, together with my friends Jan Boschman and Flo Smith. The solid snow base presented no problems when Kelly walked off the packed trail. Climbing up the ridge behind Clitheroe Meadows was a piece of cake, as the mountaineers' saying goes, although he seemed to be frequently wondering why we were so slow as we slogged up the ridge at half his pace. Skiing back down the mountain, running hard to keep up, thrilled him tremendously. Near the end of our skiing day he would become tired and contentedly trot behind, keeping pace with my skiing stride, and periodically stepping on the tails of my skis.

During this Tonquin Valley trip Kelly understood about posing for pictures and also learned that the click of the camera meant he could stop posing. My photos have been greatly enhanced by his large erect ears and sleek body, and my hiking and skiing trips are greater fun as I share his enjoyment.

While on the trail, summer or winter, it did not take Kelly long to catch on to the routine of resting at lunch break, and also my routine of bringing him two dog biscuits. As I open my lunch bag he stands in front of me, tongue hanging out, waiting for his biscuits. Finishing the second one he lies down to one side without being told, always ready to jump up with a flourish when lunch break is over.

Should you be considering taking your dog hiking or cross-country skiing, start with short hikes or ski trips. Not only do you build up the dog's stamina but your own as well. The companionship of your dog in the forest or on a mountain trail is tremendous. Many new, exciting smells and fascinating country keep dogs alert and interested. Always be aware, however, that a dog is not always welcome in many groomed ski trail areas. Pick your trail carefully when taking your dog along and I wish you many happy hours together in God's country.

Ruthie's Little Hiking Group

It all started in 2005 when Judith Chubachi was standing beside me at church giving out leaflets. Someone came to me and asked about Grotto Creek Trail. When I got home I felt very guilty that here was Judith, someone new to Canmore from the big city of Calgary who had probably never hiked before, and I hadn't invited her to go hiking. So I emailed her and asked if she wished to go hiking and she said yes right away.

We established a date and she invited Lynda Beyer along; my hiking buddy Trish Jevne from Wetaskiswin was visiting me, so she came too. We hiked up Mount Yamnuska's east shoulder. It was tough going for Judith, and I had to wait for her a few times, but she never complained. We had lunch on the top of the shoulder and enjoyed the view of the mountains and prairies. When we got back to the parking lot both Lynda and Judith said, "We should do this every week."

That was it. We did, and it evolved into every Thursday.

As time went by the group expanded with a number of people I knew, both male and female and a variety of ages.

The next year when we hiked Deer Ridge Trail in Kananaskis Country we met Franca Ponari and Maria Haines and had a friendly chat. They asked the name of our hiking group then Maria asked if I was Ruth Oltmann – she had read my book on Lizzie Rummel. Then they asked if they could join our group; so the group expanded some more and everyone got fit.

In July 2006 Elizabeth and Clarence Rabuka and Marguerite and Allen Laycock came with me to the Lake O'Hara area in Yoho National Park and we stayed in the Elizabeth Parker Hut and hiked for three days. Franca and Maria met us for a hike on our last day. By August 2006 there were twenty of us who flew into Mount Assiniboine Provincial Park for four days and just about everyone hiked to the top of The Nub at 2769 metres, among other destinations. Fourteen of us hiked the 26 km back to the cars the last day.

When winter came in 2005 I said, "Now that I've got you all fit I won't let you off the hook." So, we went cross-country skiing and snowshoeing.

During the second year of the group Judith remarked to someone: "Ruthie's going a lot slower than last year." What she didn't realize was that now she was fit she was going faster! (She is twenty years younger too.) I'd still be doing a lot of solo hikes if Judith hadn't said yes to my offer. Because she did we have both made many new friends and everyone has been to some marvellous places.

Now every May we do an anniversary hike up Mount Yamnuska's east shoulder and I take a cake to celebrate. In 2007 there were nineteen of us on this celebration hike.

There are now over twenty people on my list, although we seldom have that many on the weekly hikes. But the question now arises: Should it still be called *Ruthie's Little Hiking Group?*

Hiking Tips

Early in my mountain career while hiking to Kindersley Pass in Kootenay National Park I allowed Tom to carry my lunch in his pack and I didn't carry a pack at all. Tom was a strong hiker and he led the way. Eventually he was far ahead of the rest of us and I was running out of energy. Lunch would have been most welcome. From this episode I learned to always carry my pack and my lunch.

For safety reasons I always carry a large orange garbage bag rolled up with an elastic band around it. This works as an emergency bivi sack. I can crawl in it if I'm injured and retain body heat. Or I can give it to someone else who is in trouble. It is also very visible. It saved a young woman's life on Fortress Mountain in Kananaskis Country once as it can be seen from a helicopter. I also carry two homemade fire starters. To make them I take cardboard egg cartons and stuff them with lint from

Ruthie's Little Hiking Group at the Waterton Lakes National Park hiking camp, 2009. Left to right: Clarence and Elizabeth Rabuka, Dorle Lomas, Linda Blied, Nicole Hess (visiting from Germany), Ken Slemko, Maria and Mike Haines, Sylvia and Bruce Heebner, Val Slemko, Eric Lomas; missing: Krystyna Jahns.

my clothes dryer. When it is full I melt paraffin wax and pour it over the egg sections, then I can break off each egg section and presto, a fire starter. I also carry wind proof matches in a waterproof container, and a Swiss army knife. I take my medical cards, personal medical information, and next-of-kin names and numbers, plus my driver's license and vehicle cards. A cell phone is a recent addition. It won't always work in the mountains, but some people have had their lives saved by having one. And, or course, a first aid kit that includes Elastoplasts in a strip and a small pair of scissors as well as a triangular bandage, Tylenol and items to patch up a cut. My kit is not big, and I seldom use it on myself, but have occasionally patched up someone else. A metre of cord that can be used to repair something is a good idea. I also carry a waterproof jacket and a warm fleece, and in winter, a vest to put on when stopping for lunch. And, my number one policy is: *Never be parted from my pack.*

In an emergency people don't react the way they or you think they will. Should you be the accident victim and someone has been carrying your pack, they may decide to run off for help forgetting they have your pack. You would be stranded with none of your survival gear. Your life may depend on having those emergency items. It is important to have your pack with you even if you have to wait for a rescue. The items in it may save your life. And don't leave your pack down here while you go up there. Anything can happen between two places.

As an example of how people react, I was once hiking out of the Bugaboos after climbing Pigeon Spire with the Calgary hostel group. One of the fellows and I were ahead of our main group and while trying to be careful I slipped and broke my wrist. My friend stayed with the packs and I started hiking in a panic, as I knew a helicopter couldn't land due to the big trees we were in. I was crying and trying not to faint when I met two couples on the trail. Still weeping I said, "I broke my arm." The four of them just watched me walk by and didn't help. The trail was steep on both sides and it was with some difficulty that I tried not to faint. I kept saying to myself, "You can faint when you get to the lodge." Finally, about a half a kilometre from the end of the trail a man walking towards me saw me stagger and said, "Something wrong?" I tearfully said, "I broke my arm." He then took over and helped me to his car, gave me some pain killers and he and his family took me to Invermere hospital. He also saw to it that my friends knew what happened to me. I didn't have my pack with me and couldn't have had it due to my injury as the pack was about 35 pounds, but it is a good example of how two different groups of people reacted in an emergency. One of those four people on the trail should have tried to help me because I was alone when I passed them.

Remember, just because there are people on the trail that doesn't mean they will help you.

Chapter 10

The Best Summer of my Life

Linda Galeski, Merlene Sparks, Tom Galeski, Ruthie and Beau Galeski at the Chilkoot Trailhead in Dyea, Alaska, 2003.

Yukon and Southeast Alaska

June 1 to August 27, 2003

Email Note #1

Hi Folks:

Trees and more trees, lakes and bigger lakes, mountains and hills, they are all here and I'm enjoying myself. Talk about a relaxing time, this is it. I must dance to a different drummer because by the time I leave the sparsely populated campgrounds the roads are practically bare of traffic. I've done short walks to waterfalls and historic sites; at Jasper's Miette Hot Springs I hiked the Sulphur Skyline Trail and in Muncho Provincial Park I hiked up a little ridge. Today I walked from Miles Canyon to Canyon City before getting downtown to shop for groceries. I'm in an Internet shop and have had a lot of difficulty with the email, as there is only one Internet line into the Yukon! I am mostly staying in Yukon Territory campgrounds as they are lovely and treed. Watson Lake was practically vacant and it rained all night. Other than that I've had lovely weather. I plan to be here in Whitehorse for two or three days and then head off towards Dawson City.

Cheers & love, Ruthie

Email Note #2

Hi Everyone:

Greetings from the land of the gold rush—Dawson City, Yukon.

I'm here and it's wonderful. I've been to Mayo, Keno and at the top of Keno Hill (6066 ft.) I met a guy who had surveyed my well in Exshaw! He'd been seeing my name in the guest books in the historical places I'd visited and was anxious to meet me. He had dinner with me in my campsite in Keno City (population 15). I arrived in Dawson City on the 18th and promptly drove up the Bonanza Creek road and toured the huge Dredge #4 and drove the loop around to Hunker Creek road (all major gold rush creeks). This road is really high and the scenery is spectacular, particularly the Ogilvie Mountains to the north. Saw King Solomon's Dome and must go back to hike to the top. Read Pierre Berton's book Klondike to find out all about it. I've been touring sights in Dawson City yesterday and today. Was at a talk and reading at Robert Service's cabin and Jack London's cabin, all across the road from the Berton House where Pierre was raised. What can I write about that will allow me to be a writer in residence for three months in the Berton House? Tomorrow I leave on a three-day backpack trip down the Ridge Road Heritage Trail. The girl who checks the Klondike River Campground where I'm camping said she'd take me to the upper trailhead so I only have to hike downhill, well mostly downhill. Cheating, I know. Wednesday I fly to Inuvik with a four-hour nature trip to Tuktoyaktuk. It is so exciting being here. After thirty years of reading all the gold rush history and reading maps of the north it's hard to believe I'm here and looking at all these places. The country is so wild in spite of the gold rush dredging. It's so big. The Yukon River is big, wild, and exciting. Thanks for your messages on the 'net. I'm glad you liked the postcard Carolee. It isn't very easy to find an Internet service so my messages will be few and far between.

Email Note #3

Hi Folks:

It pays to throw caution to the winds and trust God for safety. Firstly, I did the Ridge Road Heritage Trail hike in two days instead of three. It was too short for three days. I made the first campsite in four hours—by 2:10 p.m. Now what do I do with myself when I've nothing to read? So, tent up, food bag in the tree. Check the pump—do I have to prime it? No. Thank goodness. Wander around. Read the historical sign. Write in my journal. Then in the evening I put my time to good use by praying for all and sundry. The Trinity Church folks, the family and all my friends I could think of. This took a fair bit of time and was most profitable—probably for us all. The second day I was up and at the second campsite before noon. So I had an early lunch, spent an hour reading the historical sign and recording it and events. Then down the trail to make 19.7 km in one day. Saw two grouse dragging their wings and one baby grouse rushing ahead of mom. The views from this trail are awesome—all the way north to the Ogilvie Mountains and the gold bearing hills all around. I didn't see a soul except for two runners with a dog who didn't see me, and the last kilometre of the hike when I saw three quads with four people.

The next two days were housekeeping and on Wednesday the 25th I flew to Inuvik, NWT. I made friends with a couple I met in the Dawson City terminal. No security checks here at the airport; no covered passageway to the plane, good basic flying in a smallish plane; "Everyone up front we're tail heavy." Great views looking down on the Ogilvie Mountains, the Eagle plains and the Richardson Mountains. Got set up in the Happy Valley Campground in downtown Inuvik. My minuscule tent in a corner by the mosquitoes and trees. But, hey, this campground has showers! Toured around town for the rest of the day. In particular saw the Igloo Church and learned its history from the "sister" on duty. Amazing. Had dinner at the MacKenzie Hotel. I couldn't take my backpacking stove on the plane, so had cold breakfasts and some cold lunches and dinner out. Caribou and Char.

While walking around Inuvik I went to the new hospital just because you, Krystyna, had worked in the old one. I met John Kay at the security desk and he remembers you Krystyna. He is from Old Crow and told me the best time to visit it is in August when there's lots of wildlife and blueberries. I thought about you a lot while in Inuvik, Krystyna.

The best part of this trip was like walking in Lizzie Rummel's footsteps as I flew to Tuktoyaktuk, just like Lizzie did, and had a tour of the town of 900 people, and took off my shoes and stood in the Arctic Ocean. I have a certificate to prove it too! Saw the Catholic Church that was built in 1934 on Hershel Island and moved to Tuk in 1938 (I might be a bit mixed up on dates here) and saw the log Anglican Church on its original site, built in 1938. We also got shown the entrance to the Community Ice House, a.k.a. as The Freezer. This is a 30-foot deep shaft that goes down into the permafrost with two fifty-foot tunnels going off it with compartments for people to store their meat. Particularly their caribou and whale meat as most of the town lives on these animals in the winter. Pretty amazing. We had an excellent guide. Standing on the shore of the Arctic Ocean I was overwhelmed with thoughts of Lizzie who did this in her late seventies. I think I shed a tear or two.

Getting to Tuk is a pretty awesome flight in a small plane. We all had window seats and flew only 2500 feet above the earth. A little bit of a detour to see some reindeer (I didn't see them from my vantage point). The whole flight is over the MacKenzie River delta and that is amazing. Lakes and more lakes, the Pelly River and the MacKenzie River for kilometres and kilometres. Look on a map, but seeing it for real is mind stretching and a real privilege.

So, now I am back in Dawson City getting my act together, coming back down to the ground and planning my next move. Do I go up the Dempster highway to the Tombstone Mountains or do I just head up over the Top of the World Road? I'll camp overnight and make a decision.

This trip has been better than I expected. I've met so many interesting people. Tourists just come up to you and ask where you are from and all that. The people in Inuvik mostly all say hello when they walk by you. The history in Dawson City is profound. I've seen all of the historical buildings and been to the top of The Dome twice and saw people sailing off the top. I don't know when I'll hit another Internet store, so I'll just have to touch base with you when possible.

A Top of the World Adventure

Driving towards Dawson City from the Klondike River Campground I came to a historical sign that said Hunker Creek, so I turned up the road, but the washboard was rough and I wasn't sure where I was going, so I turned back. However, the next sign I came to said Bonanza Creek. "Bonanza Creek!" I shouted to myself. I knew this was the major gold bearing creek of the Klondike Gold Rush in 1898. I couldn't help it, I turned off and made my way up the road and discovered Dredge Number Four. After an hour's tour I drove on to Discovery Claim and Eldorado Creek, but on the way there I'd seen a sign saying Upper Bonanza Creek and being the adventurous soul that I am and a mad historian, off I went. Up and up this narrow, winding road, higher and higher until I came to a picnic site with a fabulous view and the top end of the historic Ridge Road Heritage Trail. I'd read about this trail in the Yukon brochure and knew it was 32 km long, but to actually find the top end of the trail with its lovely sign and a brochure outlining the trail was like finding gold.

I also found the Upper Bonanza road hooked into the Hunker Creek Road so I took it back to the Klondike Highway. Back at the Klondike River Campground I made inquiries of the campground maintenance girl about getting a ride to the top of the Ridge Road Heritage Trail so I could leave my van at the bottom and hike downhill to it. Carol offered to take me, so a few days later I threw caution to the winds and trusted God with my life and the bears and off we went, leaving my van at the bottom end of the trail. Before leaving me at the top, Carol took my picture and then I started hiking down the trail with my backpack and three days food.

It was glorious weather and the view across the top of the hills towards the Ogilvie Mountains was spectacular, as were the views in all directions. The trail which was built in 1899 runs along a ridge between Bonanza Creek and Hunker Creek was only used until 1902 when a railway was built in another location of the ridge and ended up at what was called Soda Station. There is still an ancient boxcar at Soda Station, the part of the trail that crosses the old rail line. There is nothing left of the rail line, it's overgrown and there is nothing left of the two roadhouses along the Heritage Trail. The two backcountry campgrounds have been established where the roadhouses were with interpretive signs there and along the trail tell the story of the road. To an avid historian this was another gold mine.

I arrived at the first campground at 2:10 p.m. I found a good tree to hang my food bag in and found the pump didn't need to be primed, so I put up my wee tent, sat at the picnic table and read, wrote in my journal the information from the interpretive sign, and found a few tin artifacts in the bush. One would never know there was a roadhouse or other buildings on this site as it is now overgrown with bushes and big trees. I didn't have any serious reading material with me, so when I ran out of things to do I spent my time praying for all and sundry. My church folks, my huge family, and all the friends I could recall.

The next morning I was up and on the trail by 8:45 a.m. and arrived at the second campground in two hours—before lunch. After making notes in my journal from the interpretive sign and having an early lunch I gave up on camping there and humped down the trail back to my van at the bottom trailhead, 19.7 km altogether.

It was a marvellous hike, in lovely weather and very quiet. I saw two runners and their dog go past the first campground and no one else until I was a kilometre from the end of the trail when I saw three quads with four people.

It was That Time of the Day

Time to sit in the campground and write in my journal and read. At last I was getting to that little blue book with the red print on the cover. Words were showing up that surprised me. Words like Hunker Creek and Top of the World Highway and Dawson City. I didn't expect to find Marcia Laycock in Dawson City; after all, I had met her in Calgary at an Inscribe writers' workshop. But sitting in the Yukon River Campground this summer and reading *The Spur of the Moment* by Laycock was a whole new discovery of this quiet person. I wondered where Marcia had lived along Hunker Creek. I saw a few houses, but they looked awfully primitive. And, what were she and her husband doing in that area?

Marcia, I need to talk to you.

Email Note #4

Greetings from Haines, Alaska.

I couldn't send you a report from Whitehorse when I was last there, as I couldn't scare up Telusplanet. So, here I am in Haines and a lot has happened since I last wrote. I've spent four days (three nights) at a camp on the Kluane Icefield. In full view of—yes, I can hardly believe it myself—Mount Logan 19,850 feet (5959 metres). This was an awesome experience. I do have photos. Climbed two nunataks and got an even closer view of Mount Logan. The camp is situated on the icefield that feeds Logan Glacier, Hubbard Glacier and Kaskawulsh Glacier. I did several hikes in Kluane National Park Reserve, camping and sightseeing. Yesterday I was camping in the Yukon at Million Dollar Falls Campground (great canyon and waterfall) and then drove the Haines Highway—another spectacular experience. What a big country we live in. Now I am here for a couple of days and will head to Skagway to meet up with my Chilkoot Trail hiking companions. This morning I bumped into a guy who recognized me from Atlin! It's the hat, not the face I'm sure. I guess I forgot to tell you that I made a trip to Atlin, B.C. and toured all its historic sites, including some of the gold rush creeks. This is a very beautiful place. Atlin Lake with the sun shining on it is spectacular; especially from the top of Monarch Mountain that I hiked up. Well, enjoy yourselves. I'll report when I can.

Saint Elias Surprise

Four surgeries, two dozen broken bones, and numerous physical ailments didn't make me a likely candidate for the Saint Elias mountains, however, while on my three month touring trip through Yukon and Southeast Alaska I threw caution to the wind and flew into the Kluane Icefield with Andy Williams, a famous pilot, and his daughter Sian to her camp below Mount Queen Mary.

The 35-minute flight from the south end of Kluane Lake over the mountains and glaciers was breathtaking and spectacular as well as awe inspiring. To see the Kaskawulsh Glacier with its impressive moraines and millions of crevasses was better than a thousand pictures. During the flight I looked to the west and spotted a huge mountain, which I was told was Mount Vancouver. "Wow, Mount Vancouver! You mean I'm seeing Mount Vancouver!"

Kluane Icefield isn't the proper name, but since the icefield doesn't have one that's what Sian calls it. The Logan Glacier, two arms of the Hubbard Glacier and the Kaskawulsh Glacier all emanate from this icefield. Mount Queen Mary rises above the camp, but Queen Mary's Poodle, as the locals call it, an outlier of the main peak, hides the main part of the mountain from camp view.

When I climbed out of the airplane and looked around and saw a huge mountain in the distance, my first question was, "What's that peak?" When I was told it was Mount Logan I got so excited I kept repeating, "This is me, looking at Mount Logan; this is not a slide show!" I hadn't thought about what peaks I would see from the camp and I certainly never dreamed I'd see Mount Logan. That was for hotshot climbers, not little old maids.

Sian Williams' Quonset type tents are the sleeping accommodation and cookhouse for her camp that is situated at 8300 feet (2554 m). Thick foamies to sleep on and an extra sleeping bag to put over my two bags made for a cozy bed. The food was simple, but very good. A warm spirit of camaraderie prevailed. It was wonderful to sit on deck chairs chatting in the sun and gazing at the mountains, particularly Queen Mary's Poodle and Mount Logan. The deck chairs had to sit on a piece of plywood because the snow was so soft.

The day I arrived I was the only one with Sian in the camp. After lunch we put on snowshoes and made our way to the foot of Queen Mary's Poodle; an outstanding glaciated peak itself. Wandering up a knoll and looking back at the faint outline of the camp, barely a dot on the map, and the big gorgeous mountains shining in the sun was enormously thrilling.

The next day three other people flew into the camp. Once they got settled in their respective Quonset-type tents we all took off on snowshoes across the icefield to a nunatak in the distance. The snow is so soft and slushy, due to almost twenty-four hours of daylight, that snowshoes are a must. It is different from the Rockies summer snow that becomes firm enough to walk on. The nunatak was partially bare, so after we had lunch on the rocks at the edge of the snow we stashed the snowshoes and scrambled up the boulders to the top. I was glad I had my mountaineering boots on and not snow boots like the others as they gave me a good grip. The rock was loose with some big stable boulders and the nunatak was steeper than it looked. In among the rocks were beautiful yellow arctic poppies, bits of saxifrages and lichen. The poppies' colour is a sort of translucent yellow. From the top we were looking down the Logan and Hubbard glaciers, with great views of Mount Queen Mary, Mount King George and Mount Hub-Sew with its pointed peak, Mount Steele, Mount Augusta, as well as Mount Logan. After spending an hour on top we worked our way down and took our time snowshoeing back to camp. Every so often I would turn and look at the view of Mount Logan and the other wonderful peaks shining in the warm sun. I couldn't get enough of the scenery.

Crackers, cheese and oysters on a tray set on a barrel enabled us to stay outside while we enjoyed the panoramic view. Susan, who does ballet, fascinated me while she stood on one foot on a plastic crate balancing perfectly while taking off her over pants. It was like watching a ballet to see her. The backdrop was awesome too. During my conversation with Susan I discovered that Joyce Staples Cole (now deceased) from Canmore and Exshaw was her aunt. I had interviewed Joyce for my Kananaskis history book as her parents worked at the Rocky Mountains Park gate when Banff Park was larger than it is today and the park gate was situated just east of Exshaw. Yes, it is a small world.

On day three Sian, Doug and I snowshoed to the biggest nunatak and climbed to the top. We had to rope up on the icefield for this one as we were crossing snow covered crevasses. Among the rocks of the nunatak we found more arctic poppies and a big clump of purple flowers, possibly gentian. Lunch on the top lasted for, at least, an hour and we just enjoyed being in this marvellously beautiful place. Mount Logan, once again, dominated the view. I found it hard to take my eyes off it.

On my fourth day I woke up to total whiteout conditions, so it was a day to read, talk and relax around camp. By nine at night it started to clear and at 9:30 p.m. Andy flew in and took me back to Kluane Lake in beautiful sunshine. Gazing at all those big peaks and glaciers is awe-inspiring and it was a fitting end to my Saint Elias Mountains adventure.

No broken bones, no surgeries needed, just a wonderful, fantastic time for someone who isn't in the Mount Logan climbing category.

If you want to see the Saint Elias Mountains and you're not a big time climber check out *Icefield Discovery* at www.icefields.com. I highly recommend this unique, unforgettable experience.

Email Note #5

Greetings from Skagway, Alaska.

Done!! Yes, I've hiked the Chilkoot Trail—53.1 km. We left on July 27th and came off the trail on the 31st. What an awesome hike. Day three we woke to pouring rain and a puddle under the tent. Everything was soaked and dear Merlene carried the wet, soggy tent. (I carried the poles and pegs.) That was the day we went over Chilkoot Pass. Big, big rocks all the way up the Golden Staircase. We had to pick our way carefully up and around. Then there were two false summits and the pass is just a rock gully. Very narrow. Those gold rushers were crazy. To do that 40 times with their ton of gear is insane. Mind you they were doing it in the winter and that is easier when the rocks are covered with snow. The day we did it one guy broke his leg and had to be air lifted out. His dog was walked out with the U.S. ranger and was so exhausted it had to be kept over a day at Sheep Camp.

While I was scrambling up the pass I suddenly thought, "This is me on Chilkoot Pass!" Unbelievable. It took me six hours from Sheep Camp (our wet camp) to the summit and for someone my age (66) everyone said I was "awesome". I was relieved to get there, as those rocks were scary. There is a Canadian warden at the top and a warming hut. Since we were scrambling up in rain and wind he had hot water in thermoses for us. We rested half an hour and then had to continue another 3.75 hours to Happy Camp for the night. The Canadian side of the pass was better weather, but still very windy. It took me 9.75 hours altogether that day. A long, hard day with lots of very rocky hiking terrain.

My fourth day I was tired and it was long too, but I got my certificate (through Lynda's kindness) to say I'd hiked the Chilkoot Trail. We arrived at Bennett Lake 1.5 hours before the White Pass and Yukon Route train was to depart, so we could bone up on food. At that end of the trail there is a trail sign (an old one and a new fancy one). I took a photo of them and then promptly burst into tears. I really did the Chilkoot Trail! After thirty plus years of reading gold rush history, touring through the Yukon's gold rush sites and growing up reading Robert Service's poems this was a pretty emotional moment. All five of us in our party took the White Pass train to Fraser where the Galeski family got off to go to Whitehorse and Merlene and I continued on the train down the pass. At one point we could see a section of the old White Pass Trail. Pretty special. Wonderful views looking down big ravines and gullies and the big mountains. White Pass is 2888 feet high and Chilkoot Pass is 3525 feet. Not high by Rockies standards, but being further north, and starting from sea level, it is a different perspective. Several glaciers hanging from the higher peaks.

Merlene and I spent yesterday here in Skagway. She leaves today for Whitehorse and then Calgary. I leave here on the 5th to work my way down the Alaska panhandle to Prince Rupert. I'll be visiting some friends in B.C. as I head towards home.

This has been an unbelievable trip for me—far beyond my wildest dreams.

(Chilkoot Trail companions—Merlene Sparks (Calgary), Lynda, Tom and Beau Galeski (Bragg Creek, Alberta).

Email Note #6

Greetings from Exshaw, Alberta an obscure place in the Canadian Rockies! Yes, I arrived home yesterday evening, but only for a few days. My last travel notes are from Skagway, Alaska, and the Chilkoot Trail. Since then I took a ferry to Juneau, Alaska, where I spent five days. Camped at Mendenhall Lake Campground. I could walk twenty-five feet to the lake and look at the stunning, immense Mendenhall Glacier. Did the museums, Russian Orthodox Church, the tramway up Mount Roberts and a walk from there to Father Brown's cross, the state capital building, including a community garden with individual plots, and listened to organ music in the State Office Building at noon. Went to church and met a lady who had walked the Chilkoot Trail in one day twice! Many people actually do this and some actually run it! Amazing. I took a boat trip up Tracy Arm Fjord to the Sawyer and North Sawyer tidal glaciers. 200 feet high and 350 feet high with lots of icebergs and calving ice. When the ice calves into the sea it disturbs the shrimp, which rise to the surface, so seals and arctic terns, cormorants and gulls feed on the shrimp. Lots of 2000-foot rock walls and waterfalls and a nanny goat and her kid and an eagle's nest. Great trip.

I took a ferry from Juneau to Petersburg, via Sitka—through the Peril Strait where you could almost touch the rocks on either side of the channel. I had 3.5 hours in Sitka so saw the Russian Orthodox Cathedral (not big; lots of icons), the Russian Orthodox Bishop's house, a walk in the park along the harbour to Sheldon Jackson Museum, a bus ride back downtown, and a one-on-one tour and history of the Lutheran Church built in 1840, and an impromptu ride back to the ferry with the organist.

The great thing about these Alaskan ferries is that when you are travelling overnight you just take your Thermarest and sleeping bag and camp out in a lounge chair on the deck. Great fun and you get to meet some neat people. Some people take their freestanding tents, but I wanted the experience of being with the crowd. I had two nights on the ferry from Juneau to Petersburg via Sitka. Had three days in Petersburg, which was settled by Norwegians so there's lots of rose mailing (like folk art painting) on houses and shutters, as well as a Sons of Norway Hall. Unfortunately, I wasn't there when they put on any Norwegian dinners. Did some short walks and drove a 21-mile winding, narrow back road that was very interesting. I also walked Ohmer Creek Trail. I camped at Ohmer Creek Campground. Lovely rain forest.

I took another ferry to Wrangell, Alaska. I was there 39 years earlier to visit a friend, but this time I was able to look around. The museum was crammed and interesting. They are planning to move into better quarters. It was here that I found out about Mount Dewey Trail – I was told it was steep and difficult and I shouldn't go alone. You're right, I went. Got to the top in fifteen minutes. When I ran into the man who had told me about it the next day he asked me if I did the trail. When I said, "Yes, it was a piece of cake." He asked where I was from. When I said Banff, Alberta, he said, "Oh well, I guess it would be a piece of cake."

I also hiked to see Rainbow Falls in the rain and was part of a long survey when I got back. Whenever there is a trail in the rain forest and muskeg they make boardwalks, or planks to walk on, and stairs for the hills. Rainbow Falls had lots of planks and stairs. Lovely falls. While here I took a boat trip up the Stikine River (historic gold rush), and into Shakes Slough, Shakes Lake to Shakes tidal glacier. There are massive icebergs at the end of the lake, which were snagged on a sand bar. Our boat had to go in S-turns around the bergs. Pretty impressive. More waterfalls, an ice arch in the glacier, and big rock walls.

We stopped at one place to fish (not me) where the salmon were spawning. One slough off the main river was seventeen miles long! Thirty-nine years ago I had gone with my friends up the Stikine River to a venison roast where they roasted the deer on a spit over an open fire. While at Wrangell I camped two nights at a free forestry campground that was up on a mountainside with a fantastic view of Zamovia Strait far below. The campground was laid out in groups of three strung along this mountain forestry road. This was the nicest campground I stayed in and the price was right.

Another ferry to Ketchikan, Alaska. Saw one natural history museum. This town, like Wrangell and Juneau, is built on the side of a mountain so the roads go in two directions following the ocean or uphill very, very steeply. I took a boat tour to the Misty Fjords National Monument (similar to a park). To park my van all day I had to drive up steep streets to a parking lot and then walk down several flights of stairs with boardwalks to houses going off the stairs. Great views. Then tearing around from dock to dock, past a huge cruise ship, to find my tour boat. I made it in the nick of time. Saw whales, seals, waterfalls and fjords and, yes, misty mountains. Camped at a state campground two nights and a forestry campground one night. Walked the trail around the lake at the latter. Went to a little church and met a girl who went to Bible School in Three Hills Alberta. She thinks Ketchikan is the back of beyond.

All these towns on the Panhandle are in rainforest, naturally, so it is great to see such a different forest from the one at home. The buildings in the towns are all crammed together along the harbour and up the mountainside behind. Very steep streets, must use low gear. I always drove to the end of the roads in the two directions from the town. I encountered a fair bit of rain, but mostly at night when I was wrapped in my sleeping bag in my cocoon (a.k.a. van). I had wanted to see the Alaska Panhandle ever since I went to Wrangell in 1964, so I did it well. Unfortunately, I couldn't coordinate ferries to stay overnight in Sitka. The harbours are always full of huge, gigantic cruise ships and the shops are full of the ships' passengers. Not many of the passengers get to the museums and the outlying areas.

The last ferry was to Prince Rupert. Brother Brian lived here for a number of years. It was thirty-nine years since I was there and it is no longer a one horse town, but a thriving place. I didn't stop, except for gas, but drove east to a nice campground for the night. In Terrace I phoned Sue and Russ Wilson, but they weren't home. Drove to Telkwa, east of Smithers, and visited Hildo and Jane Hoek and their two lively grandsons, then on to Beaumont Provincial Park to camp where Martin and Sheryl Perren (formerly of Banff) came and visited me. Prince George was next, where I visited Catriona McLennan. In Quesnel I got a new signal light bulb and did a laundry, phoned Albert Skretka, but he wasn't home, however, he got my message and forewarned his dad in Kamloops that I was heading his way. At 108 Mile House I visited Barrie and Anne Bolton and their daughter Victoria and son-in-law Gabe. Kamloops was a visit with Ed and Marie Skretka and Ruth Whittiker. En route to Armstrong I drove through the Falkland forest fire area and visited Don and Mary Campbell and Yvonne, Geoff and Tim Spedding. On to Rogers Pass to camp and visit ACC folks at Wheeler Hut. In Canmore I stopped to see Bill and Lucille Pulliam and discuss the next trip and bought groceries.

This three-month trip was totally awesome; far better than I could ever have imagined. I am very grateful to my praying friends and family. My only injury was Achilles tendonitis in one foot from the Chilkoot Trail's 90 per cent rock. It is almost better, but I did limp around Southeast Alaska.

Montana, Wyoming & Colorado

September 1 - 15, 2003

The following trip took place four days after I arrived home from the north. Bill and Lucille Pulliam were the leaders.

Email Note

Hi Everyone:

At last I am home to stay. The big travels are over.

For this latest excursion, I left home on September 1st and drove through Kananaskis and met up with four other folks in two vans at Highwood

Junction. We then met in Waterton Lakes National Park and camped at Belly River Campground. From there we worked our way to Great Falls, Montana, and toured the Charlie Russell Museum. Fabulous paintings; not only by Russell, but also other artists, as well as sculptures. What talent. At that point two people departed our company due to a health problem and three of us continued in two vans, down through Montana to Chico Springs hot springs (lovely), through Thermopolis and the Wind River Canyon which is fabulous. This canyon is 14 miles long, 1.3 to 2 miles across and 2400-foot high cliffs and the road runs through it. Simply amazing. We ended up in Yellowstone National Park from the north and went southeast through the Beartooth Mountains. We camped here four nights and saw three huge herds of bison; hiked to Beauty Lake twice, first from one direction and then from another direction. Ending up at either end of the lake each time.

Marvellous lakes on the High Lakes Trail. We were camping at 9518 feet. We followed the Beartooth Mountains with the road winding through Montana and Wyoming and rising over 10,000 feet. We ended up at Red Lodge, Montana for lunch, laundry and groceries. Back again to our campsite in the Beartooth Mountains. Pretty awesome road engineering I must say. Fabulous views. Then down the Chief Joseph Highway and up over the Nez Perce Pass—more awesome scenery—ending up in Colorado where we did a big horseshoe drive in Rocky Mountains Park on the Trail Ridge Road which is 12,183 feet high at its highest point. At the visitor centre we hiked up 200 feet to a great viewpoint. A pretty amazing place. We finally ended up at Bill and Lucille's cabin in Allenspark, Colorado, where we recovered. We did two day hikes here—one to a waterfall and the other to Isabelle Lake at about 11,000 plus feet. The treeline in Colorado is about 10,500 feet or so. (Canadian Rockies tree line is 7500 feet). One evening I drove to Lyons, Colorado, and met up with Jim Magee (former hosteller from Ribbon Creek, now living in Boulder), his wife Mary and young son Jamy. We had a picnic supper and a visit.

On Friday, September 12th, I left Bill and Lucille and headed home. I spent a day going south through another big canyon (I avoided the gross casinos in Black Hawk town), then east and north into Wyoming. At one point I followed a "good gravel road", which after three days of rain wasn't all that good, but the scenery of rolling hills and the huge Three Forks Ranch was very pretty. In Wyoming I toured Grand Teton National Park and did a big counter clockwise loop in Yellowstone National Park to see the Grand Canyon of Yellowstone, mud pots, various geysers and Old Faithful. My timing was so perfect I only waited twenty minutes to see Old Faithful strut his stuff. Pretty impressive and quite amazing.

From there I headed to West Yellowstone to camp and from that point on I made a beeline for home in two long days. My last night camping was in Choteau, Montana. I had gone north a bit past Choteau, but when I hit a snowstorm and saw a motor home pass me shedding snow, I turned back to the KOA Kampground in Choteau. The better part of valour I thought. The shower was nice too. The next day I was grateful I had turned back when

I saw all the snow on the ground further north. I avoided Chief Mountain border crossing due to the snow and came into Canada at Carway, just south of Cardston. Lunch was at Waterton Dam and north through Pincher Creek, Highway 22 and into Kananaskis Country.

Driving north in Kananaskis, looking at the spectacular snow covered mountains I realized that really, Kananaskis is the prettiest place I've been— well, Mount Logan area is beside it for beauty. After driving 610 km I arrived home at 6:00 p.m. last night, unloaded the van, checked my mail and my forty-four e-mail messages, had dinner and collapsed into bed.

I've had a fabulous once-in-a-lifetime summer. I've taken photos of the backcountry, but very few of the front country, but I have a ten-pound box of brochures to remind me, a journal with copious notes, and great memories.

Happy trails, Ruthie

Summer of Freedom

Why was it the best summer of my life? Because I went on this Yukon/SE Alaska trip alone (other than hiking the Chilkoot Trail). I could do what I wanted, when I wanted, and no one whined saying, "I don't want to see another museum," or complained that they didn't want to do "that"—I didn't have to compromise on what I did. I went to places that were of great interest to me, like the camp in the Icefield of the Saint Elias Mountains, Inuvik, and Tuktoyaktuk and every museum I came across. It was a summer free from worries and responsibilities. It was a summer of total freedom, exciting adventures, beautiful scenery, and fascinating places. Something that rarely happens in anyone's life.

On the second trip Bill and Lucille were expert, knowledgeable leaders in an area I would not have ventured alone. They introduced me to stunning scenery, beautiful hikes and some of America's amazing places.

Epilogue

Ruthie with wheels on Marl Lake Trail, Peter Lougheed Provincial Park, 2010.

My Life on the Trail

There are many noble peaks in the Canadian Rockies and while I've never been a big-time mountain climber, I have had the thrill of climbing a few of these peaks. Mostly I've been a hiker and backcountry skier and also recently a snowshoer. I've done many wonderful multi-day backcountry hikes, and have hiked and/or skied about 85-90 per cent of the trails in Canada's four mountain parks and Kananaskis Country, as well as many places without trails, and a few other regions in Canada. I've had the privilege of skiing glaciers and icefields and been to so many marvellous places it has been like a dream.

I've met hundreds of people while in the mountains and I frequently meet people I know while on a trail. My life has been enriched immeasurably by where I've been and the people I've met and know I'd be the poorer without them.

Like any human being I've made some mistakes and I've done some things right. I've had heartbreaking moments in my life, so there are a few things I don't want to re-live, but there are some I do, and there are many mountain places I would like to revisit. I can't carry a big backpack any more, but I can still get out hiking, cross-country skiing, snowshoeing and travelling and add to my adventures in different ways. I still love pottering in the kitchen baking bread and cookies, and digging in the garden. I'm still involved with the Alpine Club of Canada, my church, and now the *Heart Mountain Go-Getters* (Exshaw seniors). *Ruthie's Little Hiking Group* is still going strong in spite of the fact that during most of 2010 and into 2011, I couldn't hike due to my back problem. I

Tanya (Mark), Jill (Katie) and Jack the dog, Nicole (Ezralynn and Ohlund), Laura (Caleb), and Menaka (Theron) in Bow Valley Provincial Park, 2010.

organize the hikes and snowshoeing, meet the group and see them off at the trailheads. Also as a result of my back problem another group has emerged. *Hikers with Wheels* consists of young moms with tots and toddlers in strollers and me with my wheeled walker using paved trails in Kananaskis. Although I have to walk for a few minutes and then sit down and repeat this over and over the moms are very enthusiastic. Hopefully the walker will be retired soon, but this group will continue.

It has been a rewarding life and I am grateful to God for his guidance and care, and in looking back I consider myself rich. Not in money, but in experiences and in the amazing, spectacular places I've seen, and the wonderful people I've met and known. It has all been a tremendous gift. Never in my wildest dreams would this skinny kid from Ottawa have imagined this life of great adventure.

Don't Fence Me In

Oh, give me land lots of land under starry skies above,
Don't fence me in.
Let me hike through the wide-open country that I love,
Don't fence me in.
Let me be by myself in the evening breeze,
Listen to the murmur of the evergreen trees.
Send me off forever, but I ask you please,
Don't fence me in.
Just turn me loose, let me hike in my old boots underneath the mountain skies.
On my two feet, let me wander over yonder 'til I see the mountains rise.
I want to hike to the ridge where the snow commences.
Gaze at the moon 'til I lose my senses.
Can't look at cities and I can't stand fences,
Don't fence me in.

Adapted from the song Don't Fence Me In.